ADVANCE PRAISE

"Annie Burnside's teachings are infused with universal truths that can heal our lives and spark a major shift in consciousness. Her enlightening and soul-stirring work is a must-have on your bookshelf."

> **MICHAEL J. CHASE**, best-selling author of *Am I Being Kind* and *The Radical Practice of Loving Everyone*

"Annie Burnside has done it again. I deeply appreciated her blend of wisdom, gentleness, and humanness in her first book, *Soul to Soul Parenting*. I gave a copy to all my kids. Now in her new book, *From Role to Soul*, she has brought her truth forward for all, not just parents, in a collection of easy-to-read, stand-alone essays. Annie cuts through the linguistic maze of religion versus spiritual paths right to the chase. She points out significant shifts that help us realize we are whole and complete right now, if we only recognize it."

> **JILL SCHRODER**, author of *BECOMING: Journeying Toward Authenticity*

"*From Role to Soul* takes us on a journey into authenticity, through which we not only come to know our own deepest self, but by so doing become truly available to life—for our children, our spouse, our work, and our interests. While at times we have to fulfill roles, they can too easily become an identity that forms a huge block between ourselves and the person we want most to benefit from our presence in their life. The trick is to become true to ourselves in every aspect of our life, which automatically resonates with everyone and everything we are involved with. Annie shows us how she did it, and the wonderful difference it made in her life and that of the many people she touches."

> **SHEFALI TSABARY, PH.D.**, clinical psychologist and author

"We are all connected. It's whether we choose to be conscious of this connection that's the issue. Not being aware of our connectedness is like circumnavigating the globe assuming it to be flat. I love Annie's inspired work as she helps others to appreciate connection. Her message is so human and at the same time divine. Annie teaches from this perspective, and this is the power of her teaching—the power of truth."

    MIKE VECCHIO, author of *ICE, India & Old Lovers*

"Annie plays a wonderful host as she invites us all to experience our own journey to self discovery. She'll pique your curiosity and tease out what your heart has always known, but your head may not be clear. In her wonderful Annie way, she shows us that life is less about taking a side and more about accepting the whole. Annie makes you think you're discovering yourself with a close friend rather than some guru, and that works for me!"

    JOSH BECKER, founder of www.isimply.am

"Whether you're looking for a soul nurturer or an opportunity to simply broaden your perspective on life, Annie has that to offer and so much more. With her gentle facilitation skills, open heart, humor and genuine 'Annieness' she is a powerful mirror, guidepost and friend to all whom she encounters. If you have the opportunity to be in her presence or read her books, your life (and the lives of those around you) will be enriched beyond measure!"

    KAY MCBREARTY, Soul to Soul Circle participant

"Annie Burnside is an incredible spiritual teacher and human being. She radiates joy and love and makes spirituality accessible and understandable to all. It was Annie who 'introduced' me to God—and I will forever be grateful."

    JENNIFER BEACOM, Soul to Soul Circle participant

"Annie is a teacher who is warm, knowledgeable and insightful. Her very accessible teaching style provides a safe and nurturing environment for her students to safely share and be vulnerable. Much of Annie's success comes from her passion for the subject matter and her exquisite ability and willingness to share examples from her own life as teaching tools. She radiates love, light, compassion and empathy; in other words, she walks the walk!"

    GERI KIRKPATRICK, Soul to Soul Circle participant

"Annie is an honest, kind, funny, loving, and authentic person. Her Soul to Soul Circles are exactly the same. She has enlightened me to so many new ways of thinking and approaching life. She sparks something in your soul and leaves you wanting to know more about living an authentic life. My favorite thing about Annie is her passion. She has such enthusiasm for life and for teaching others how to live a soul to soul life. Her passion is very catchy because you can see what joy and happiness it brings to her everyday. Annie is truly a blessing to anyone she encounters."

    SALLY CHRIST, Soul to Soul Circle participant

"I smile to myself, knowing it was a divine wink that brought Annie into my life as a spiritual advisor and teacher. However, I never feel 'taught to' by Annie. Working with her is as comfortable as an intimate huddle together with my sisters. In effect, Annie is a sister to all the women who have shared a moment, a conversation, a book or a class with her. There is wisdom that reaches my soul, as well as practical everyday ideas that every mother, sister, daughter, wife, and girlfriend can use. Annie quickly became a key touchstone in my life!"

    SARAH PURCELL, Soul to Soul Circle participant

FROM ROLE to SOUL

15 Shifts
ON THE
Awakening Journey

FROM ROLE TO SOUL

15 Shifts ON THE Awakening Journey

ANNIE BURNSIDE
Award-Winning Author of *Soul to Soul Parenting*

Wyatt-MacKenzie Publishing
DEADWOOD, OREGON

DEDICATION

I dedicate this book to all those willing and ready to utilize their own unfolding life to awaken.

From Role To Soul
15 Steps on the Awakening Journey

F I R S T   E D I T I O N

ISBN: 978-1-939288-57-8
Library of Congress Control Number: 2014939687

©2014 Annie Burnside

All rights reserved. No part of this book may be reproduced in any manner whatsoever without written permission except in the case of brief quotations embodied in critical articles and reviews.

Edited by David Ord
Proofread by Karen Kibler

Soul to Soul Parenting® is a registered trademark.

"She Let Go" ©Safire Rose. Used by permission.

For information on quantity discounts, wholesale orders, and rights contact:
nancy@wyattmackenzie.com

Wyatt-MacKenzie Publishing
DEADWOOD, OREGON

www.wyattmackenzie.com

Contents

"She Let Go" xi
Foreword xiii

Part I
What Is "Awakening"?

This Isn't the Book I Thought I Was Going to Write 1
What Does it Take to Awaken? 8
Living Free 13
The Shifts 23

Part II
15 Steps to Awakening

1 From Role to Soul 33
    From Identification to Wholeness
    From Ego to Soul
    From Personality to Core
    From False-Self to True-Self
    From Character to Actor

2 From Path to No Path 44
    From Straight Line to Circle
    From Adding to Shedding
    From Knowledge to Awareness
    From Complexity to Simplicity

3 From Outer Symptoms to Inner Signals 54
    From Limited Connection to Body to Intimacy with
    Intelligent System
    From Doctor Tell Me to Body Tell Me
    From Physical Layer to Energetic Layer
    From Literal to Symbolic

4 From Woe Is Me to Grow Is Me 72
    From Dark Night to Increased Light
    From Exterior to Interior

From Denial to Trusting the Trigger
From Shadow to Illumination
From Embedding Emotions to Feeling Emotions Fully

5 From Busyness Without to Stillness Within 83
From Compulsive Mind Chatter to Deep Listening
From Perpetual Action to Thoughtful Action
From Near-Constant Doing to More Frequent Being
From Non-stop Talking to Intentional Hearing

6 From Hiding to Self-Expression 94
From Restraint to Freedom
From Holding Back to Vulnerability
From Masks to Authenticity
From Fear to Courage
From Imposed Arenas to Natural Gateways
From Ego Needs to Soul Preferences

7 From Striving to Contentment 108
From Trying to Simply Breathing
From Struggle to Relaxation
From Holding On to Letting Go
From Attachment to Surrender
From Planned Strategies to Organic Growth
From Project Motivation to Soul Calling
From Needing a Timetable to Trusting the Process
From Long-term Goals to Spontaneity

8 From Back End Awareness to Front End Awareness 116
From Blame to Accountability
From Unconsciousness to Presence
From Randomness to Mindfulness
From Rigidity to Flow
From Lack of Discrimination to Discernment
From Reacting to Reality to Creating Reality
From Coincidence to Synchronicity

9 From Self-Betrayal to Self-Love 129
From People-Pleasing to Boundaries

From Self-Sabotage to Freedom
From False Humility to True Power
From Subconscious Code to Soul Code
From Diplomacy to Truth
From Indirect to Forthright

10 From Extreme Empathy to True Service 138
From Merging With Another's Darkness to Simply Shining Light
From Half Love to Higher Love
From Enabling to Helping
From Saving Another to Inviting Another
From Doing to Modeling

11 From Diminishment to Mutuality 149
From Competition to Space for All
From Intimidation to Ownership
From Expert to Equal
From Teacher/Student to Two Souls
From Hidden Agenda to Transparency
From Comparison to Self-Acceptance
From Should to Either Partake or Pass
From Giving Away Power to Empowerment

12 From Resisting the Paradoxes to Resting Within Them 162
From One Perspective to Many
From Either-Or to Both-And
From Highs and Lows to Equanimity
From Judgment to Observation
From Anxiety to Gratitude
From Labeling to Neutrality

13 From the Little Love to the Big Love 172
From Role to Role to Soul to Soul
From Judgment to Compassion
From Non-Forgiveness to Loving Them Anyway
From Closed Heart to Open Heart
From Hardness to Softness

14 From Individuation to Oneness 183
   From Separation to Unification
   From Literal to Multi-Dimensional
   From Finite to Infinite
   From Limited to Unlimited
   From Duality to Non-Duality
   From Death to No-Death

15 From Physical Being to Blended Being 195
   From Compartmentalization to Integration
   From Societal Norms to Soul Resonance
   From Another's Truth to One's Own Truth
   From Uncertainty to Trust
   From Unease to Gratitude
   From Constraints to Freedom
   From Ego Orientation to Conscious Spirit
      Embodiment
   From Half to Whole

Final Thoughts 205

APPENDIX I 213
   A Self-Love Kit

APPENDIX II 216
   Pillars of Wisdom for the World of Education

APPENDIX III 217
   Soul to Soul Circles

INDEX 223

She Let Go
Safire Rose

She let go. Without a thought or a word, she let go.

She let go of the fear. She let go of the judgments. She let go of the confluence of opinions swarming around her head. She let go of the committee of indecision within her. She let go of all the "right" reasons. Wholly and completely, without hesitation or worry, she just let go.

She didn't ask anyone for advice. She didn't read a book on how to let go. She didn't search the scriptures. She just let go.

She let go of all of the memories that held her back. She let go of all of the anxiety that kept her from moving forward. She let go of the planning and all of the calculations about how to do it just right. She didn't promise to let go. She didn't journal about it. She didn't write the projected date in her Day-Timer. She made no public announcement and put no ad in the paper. She didn't check the weather report or read her daily horoscope. She just let go.

She didn't analyze whether she should let go. She didn't call her friends to discuss the matter. She didn't do a five-step Spiritual Mind Treatment. She didn't call the prayer line. She didn't utter one word. She just let go.

No one was around when it happened. There was no applause or congratulations. No one thanked her or praised her. No one noticed a thing. Like a leaf falling from a tree, she just let go.

There was no effort. There was no struggle. It wasn't good and it wasn't bad. It was what it was, and it is just that.

In the space of letting go, she let it all be. A small smile came over her face. A light breeze blew through her. And the sun and the moon shone forevermore.

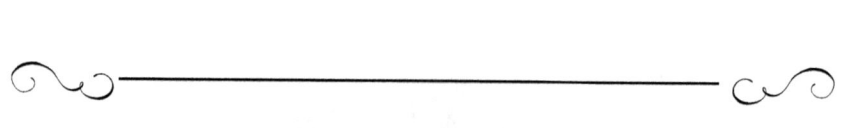

Foreword

Imagine you grow up a little more sensitive than most. You are keenly aware of others, a people pleaser, someone who likes to keep everyone else's interests in mind. Not only that, but you "feel" other people when they are around—you actually sense their feelings and recognize what they may need to hear.

As you mature, you realize most people have strong opinions, but you can't help but see every side of an argument. You struggle to see black and white, because everything just seems gray. How can we tell others what to do when we haven't walked in their shoes? How can anyone expect us all to think alike or be the same when each of us has a different history and experiences?

Seeing gray as an adult may be viewed as a skill; but when you are young, it feels weak. It feels indecisive, as if you have no position. So you go through the world unsure of what you stand for, feeling the weight of other people's discomfort and fear.

And the uncomfortable feelings of others are confusing and unsettling, because deep down inside, you know everything is okay and everybody is good. Of course there are challenges, issues, pain, but you know we are safe and that love is always available.

But you can't speak these words because you sound crazy. How do you explain to others that we are all connected, all have a voice and purpose, and that love is the only thing that matters?

How do you do this when everyone tells you that education and money are the keys to success, that competition makes you worthy, that hiding your feelings and vulnerability makes you strong?

This disparity between internal beliefs and external demands leads to insecurity, fear, and even depression.

You feel the need to hide yourself, do what others tell you to do, listen to voices that claim they have the answer.

Then one day you recognize you've had enough. You've experienced enough pain not being yourself. You've carried too much of other people's pain. You've bought into too many painful stories about the world. And you begin to read and discover there are others like you. You find other "seekers," other people who are looking for a more authentic way of being. You shift your focus from the negativity of the external world to the beauty of a more heart-centered viewpoint.

You read all the books, you take all the classes, you attend all the workshops, and you admire all of the teachers.

Then one day you recognize, to your dismay, that you are walking a similar path as before. You are following the words of others. You feel you need to please others or demonstrate how you are supporting their beliefs. You are, yet again, seeking that vicious cycle of approval.

Then you wake up and realize that while you've been educating yourself and filling up on other people's knowledge, you've forgotten to listen to yourself. You've forgotten to honor what feels good to you—forgotten to live your own story.

Then you recognize that your history, your family, your teachers, and your external influences were perfect. They were exactly the way they were supposed to be. And now you get to decide how you process these influences—what you take in and what you let go of. You get to decide what you call "true."

You realize that you can live an authentic and internally driven life, and simultaneously honor everyone else's choices. You can accept your humanness, and instead of trying to push away the world, discover ways to appreciate, live, and thrive within it.

Then imagine you meet someone who instinctively

relates to your story and shares an incredibly similar history. Imagine talking to someone who uses the same language, who relates to your stages of learning, who understands your way of being.

That was my experience when I met Annie Burnside. Annie was out promoting her first book when my mom caught one of her interviews on the radio. She called me immediately and said, "I heard an interview this morning, and this woman's book is similar to yours. She sounded just like you."

I reached out to Annie and was delighted to find we both lived in the suburbs of Chicago. We met for the first time and recognized that although we just met, we already knew each other: the stories, the path, the pain, the familiar yet unpredictable road to awakening.

While we understand and relate to each other on a profound level, we express ourselves in different ways. I tend to consider myself "ground level"—helping kids and adults embrace their authentic selves, whereas Annie invites us to take life a step further, see beyond our identification and roles, recognize our greater connection, embrace our limitlessness.

I understand Annie's belief system, but she *embodies* her belief system. Her writing, teachings, and choices demonstrate her understanding of the bigger picture of life—a faithfulness to what's felt rather than seen.

Annie encourages me, and so many others, to just trust myself, to be myself. She is nothing other than herself, and her expectation of others is the same. It's rare to find a person who supports and cheers for you when you share your joys, while simultaneously holding space for you when you share the darker and more vulnerable parts of yourself.

Annie deeply values her own experience, yet embraces the fact that everyone's experience is different. She knows there is not one way, no "right" answer to questions.

There is only individual experience—and at the same time, there is only *one*. Annie is an enthusiast of paradox, and she knows that both light and dark have balanced value.

I often tell Annie that we were made from the same stardust. I'm so appreciative of our closeness and our shared ideals. I know she agrees and appreciates our friendship. I also know she views us and everything else in much bigger terms.

To Annie, it isn't just about us; it's about all. We are all from the same, we are all connected. We are all one. Our friendship makes connection seem easy, but in this book Annie asks us to see beyond what's "easy," and to recognize and relate beyond our families, our roles, our identifications, and just know that we are literally all in this together.

This book is her journey, and she wouldn't expect you to relate to all of her experiences. She would rather have you reflect on your own experiences, to recognize the value and rightness of your own life.

Her words and experiences can act as a gateway to your own. This book is not a "how to." It's an opportunity to tap into your own self-understanding. Annie opens her heart and shares her intimate story not to convince, but to help you ignite your desire to dig deeper and go on your own personal journey.

Picking up this book is the beginning of a fabulous adventure. Allow Annie's words to shine a light on your true self, on your personal road to wholeness.

That's how she inspires everyone she meets, and that's the gift she continually gives me. I am so grateful that she reminds me to look inside and see beyond my perceived limitations.

I know you will soon feel the same.

Cathy Cassani Adams, Co-Founder Be U, Inc.
Author of *The Self-Aware Parent*

PART I

What Is "Awakening"?

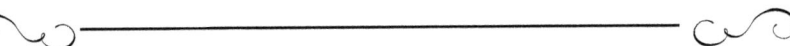

PART 1

1

This Isn't the Book I Thought I Was Going to Write

"I'M A LIFELONG SEEKER," SAID A WOMAN TO A FRIEND of mine. For this individual, as for many, to be a seeker is a badge of honor. It certainly was for me for many years. But I've pretty much dropped the label "spiritual" these days. I'm just interested in being *who I am,* true to myself in every aspect of my life.

This unifying of our lives is something most religious traditions regard as the farthest inner frontier toward which a human can journey. For most of us it's considered largely unachievable in this life, whereas what I've discovered is that it's the way each and every day can and *should* be lived.

To think of myself as a seeker was a huge blind spot of mine for many years. It kept me from awakening, since I was always trying to get somewhere and be something different from what I was. Such a mindset generates much judgment, both of ourselves and others. We live with a constant feeling of inadequacy. This sense of inadequacy promotes separation from our true state, which is inherently a wholeness in which we feel at peace with ourselves and fulfilled.

In other words, *to be a seeker is the opposite of what awakening is all about.*

And yet, it is *also* true that for many, including me, it took being a seeker to understand that it's not necessary. And the same is true of having role models, which I mention below.

I recognize there are no role models out there for me anymore. I now look at others solely as fellow souls sharing perspective and experience. After almost twenty-five years as a spiritual seeker, the knowing that began to form within me toward the end of my time on the spiritual path finally took root. I came to see that it's just "me," in a universal oneness that's the source of everything, finally coming to the place I can live my life quite simply *as I am.* It's as straightforward and as complex as that.

In a nutshell, I stopped trying to be spiritual and instead moved towards becoming fully, truly, unabashedly *myself.*

The Missing Piece (Peace)

You'll get a quick picture of the journey I've taken if I tell you that, originally, the title of this book was going to be *The Missing Piece (Peace).* It was to be supremely focused on all things spiritual, as I was for many years.

My life and work used to revolve around the missing piece—the missing *peace*—in my life. And not just in my life, but in the lives of others and of our world as a whole. There is indeed a missing piece that's the reason so many of us don't enjoy inner peace. The strange thing is that few of us who think of ourselves as seekers are bold enough to look at this missing piece head-on—even though it's the key to our own inner peace, peace in our relationships, and peace as a planet.

This piece I speak of isn't a religious piece, a political piece, an economic piece, a cultural piece, or an educational piece. Nations repeatedly look to the latest political messiah, some new economic reform, a revolutionary social movement, or improved education as the "answer" to the missing piece. But no matter how intensely we focus our personal and global energies on these aspects of our existence, the peace we long for both as individuals and as a world has never, and will never, come about by piecing our fragmented lives together through any of these channels. Neither will we ever be able to piece together our fragmented world by means of conferences, resolutions, fresh initiatives, and still another round of peace talks.

Realizing that religion, politics, economics, social organizations, and education don't hold the answer, like so many of us I imagined the missing piece to be spiritual. It may seem strange then that today I no longer prefer the term spiritual. The problem is that too often it implies something other than our everyday human existence. Instead, I prefer to speak of *wholeness*—a wholeness grounded in a maturity within our interior landscape that relatively few adults, as of yet, typically choose.

Wholeness implies authenticity, personal truth, an awareness of our ultimate oneness—both within ourselves and with everyone and everything else. It involves the ability to be truly present in heart and mind in whatever we may be doing. Sadly, this isn't the way most of us live. Instead of enjoying wholeness, we experience ourselves as a diminished version of our true being.

Does it not seem strange that if we ever stop to think of ourselves as more than we presently know ourselves to be, it's usually in terms of something we hope to *eventually* become, perhaps in an afterlife?

Such a view of ourselves leaves us far short of ever living out our potential in this life. In a sense, it keeps us more like children than adults, in that we never really take responsibility for living fully. We may appear to be adults—forty, fifty, sixty, or more years of age—and yet many of us are stuck in an undeveloped interior landscape befitting that of a child. In fact, a lot of children enjoy a greater sense of fulfillment, expressing themselves more fully, than many an adult. The vast majority of us have simply never connected with who we *really* are as intuitive, creative, powerful beings—humans who are intrinsically "soul."

Oops. Did I say "soul"? Since this isn't in any way a religious book, I need to clarify why I'm using such a word, and to point out that there's nothing religious—not that I'm *against* religion in any way—about, for instance, *soul food* or *soul music*. They are expressions that have to do with experiencing deep *feelings,* not religious dogma.

Early in my career, I thought about backing away from talking about soul so that what I have to share might be more appealing to the mainstream. The problem is, my work would then lack integrity. I am who I am, where I am on my journey, and this is how I speak and therefore how I write. It's also how I live. My message is deep, soft, gentle, and direct—and so am I as a person. What I have to share speaks to the heart more than to the mind.

Having said this, I don't want you to think of "soul" in terms of just feelings. Soul *is* deeply feeling, but it's also an expression of the depth dimension of reality itself. It speaks of our *essential* being, which is far more than any of us yet know ourselves to be. What *I* mean by "soul," which is quite different from what churches, for instance, tend to mean, will really only emerge as we proceed.

What Are You, Really?

When I use the word "soul" to refer to our essential beings, I need to be clear that I'm not talking about the traditional religious idea of an immortal soul housed in a mortal body. Much of religion subscribes to the idea that some aspect of us we aren't terribly familiar with, but which is generally referred to as our "soul," goes on when we die, and that the state *beyond* death ought therefore to be the focus of a spiritual life.

The question I wish to ask is: what do we mean when we say, "When *we* die?" Who is the "we" that we imagine dies?

If we examine the statement "when we die," the "we" to which we are referring is our body, heart, and mind. As for our "soul," as I mentioned above, it's assumed to be some element in us we really know little about—and in most people's view *won't* know about until we no longer have a body. In other words, soul is for most of us a sort of afterthought, something for beyond this life.

I'm saying that "we" don't ever die, but that only the way we have chosen to express ourselves in this lifetime on this particular planet is what dies, and it does so only in order to give rise to a further expression of our essential being. So when I speak of soul, I'm referring to who we are in our essence expressing itself in the form of our humanness.

Soul isn't something housed in a body that's alien to our human existence. Rather, the body is an *expression* of soul, though not its *ultimate* reality. The formless is expressing as form, which is fundamentally different from the dualistic idea that soul and our physical form are entirely separate, with the one housed temporarily in the other. Although our physical form is relative, whereas soul is absolute, neither is contrary to the other—unlike what much of religion has too often insisted over the centuries.

It's important to appreciate the difference between seeing soul as something "housed" in a body and seeing our embodied state as an *expression* of ourselves as soul. I can't emphasize enough that the two concepts are fundamentally opposed—the first dualistic, the second holistic. From a dualistic mindset, the body is regarded as a necessary evil that has to be "put up with" for a time, rather than being seen as soul's way of experiencing itself. Consequently, many of us have bought into an understanding of ourselves in which our "bodiliness" is regarded with suspicion, as if somehow being a disembodied spirit is the ideal. Is it any wonder we feel at war with ourselves much of the time? Split into pieces like this, there's zero chance for inner peace, let alone peace in our larger life.

To understand ourselves as soul expressing in human form *is* the missing piece, the gateway to wholeness. We remember, recognize, and acknowledge ourselves as a blending of soul and the earth's elements, whereby soul manifests itself *as* our human state. Unlike what most religious people believe, as well as many who think of themselves as on a path that's "spiritual but not religious," there's absolutely no duality in our humanness. Body, mind, and heart are simply what soul looks like in human form.

Why We Don't Need to "Fix" Ourselves

Since our lives have become fragmented, how are we to integrate the fragmented pieces, thereby restoring the inner peace with which we've lost touch?

Integration occurs as we allow soul, which is our essence, to inform every aspect of our daily lives. As everything we do becomes increasingly guided by the oneness at the heart of our being, we find ourselves no longer thinking of ourselves in terms of being "wounded" by our childhood and subsequent events. This is accompanied by the uncovering of hidden beliefs imparted by others but that no longer serve us well, which we then shed in favor of *our* truth. We also find ourselves owning emotions we may have long denied—emotions we were perhaps told weren't "spiritual" or "godly." As we learn to feel *all* the emotions humans are capable of experiencing, we undergo a clearing of our psychic debris, which leads both to inner peace and to joyful external self-expression.

It's vital to understand that, rather than trying to "fix" ourselves by repairing our fragmented parts, we are simply allowing our various fragmented pieces to be drawn together again and reunited into a whole. The opposite of fixing ourselves, this occurs spontaneously as we dive deeper into an awareness of the intrinsic oneness of our being, which encompasses awareness of the greater oneness that expresses itself as the whole of existence.

In other words, wholeness arises quite naturally from discovering our *core* as *soul*. It's about coming to know and fully embrace the manner in which who we essentially are seeks to express itself in our everyday lives. Simply put, we find ourselves becoming *comfortable in our own skin.*

We've already seen that if we had a religious upbringing, it's likely we learned early in life *not* to feel all that comfortable in our own skin. "Soul" was taught as positively contrary to our humanity with its appetites and inclinations. Our desires were seen as suspect and almost certainly opposed to the "will of God." Many of us learned to believe that if we enjoyed something, it must be wrong!

If we truly desire peace within and without, it begins with an awareness that our existence as humans isn't contrary to our essence as soul, but that our humanness is the precious expression of soul. All the other things we may engage in to improve our lives are secondary to this realization, including the paths we may walk.

PART 1

2

What Does It Take to Awaken?

AWAKENING CAN SEEM DAUNTING AND OUT OF REACH for many of us, but in reality awakening is simply an expanded lens through which we view our life's experiences. This expanded lens comes about as an organic process that unfolds in a unique way for each individual, albeit with similar threads.

It may surprise you to hear that we can awaken to inner truth at any moment. How can this be? For the simple reason that *everything* exists in the oneness, whose center is everywhere. We can never be separate from this oneness, and therefore never separate from our center. It's a question only of opening our eyes. For this reason, awakening spontaneously at what might seem like a most unlikely moment—without all the hard work required by the various paths—is always a possibility. Indeed, it happens!

It turns out that to awaken, we don't necessarily need more teachings—let alone dark nights and painful symptoms to "learn" from. For this reason, I want to stress that we don't need to be spiritual, religious, metaphysical, or mindful to awaken to who we are and begin living a peaceful, joyous, and fulfilling life.

Religion, metaphysics, meditation, mindfulness, yoga,

jogging, walking in nature, chanting—all can serve as valid paths. But even as they can be a benefit to becoming whole, they can also be an impediment. If we see our paths as temporary vehicles, there's far less chance we'll become stuck on a specified path—stuck in the role of a "seeker." Being a seeker as I was for so many years, ever on the lookout for a new teaching—and at times, wallowing in the pain of dark nights—can actually delay awakening.

While for some of us there may be a learning curve that's utilized and even enjoyed sometimes for years, it may surprise you to hear that you don't need a ritualistic, sacrificial, book-filled, workshop-full, or meditation-oriented daily routine to make headway in awakening. While certain paths and practices can be helpful for a time, they often become less and less needed as our awakening expands—as our self-focus flips from outer to inner, which then blends back into how we see the entirety of our lives and the world. Awakening is all about blending our inner being and outer reality, which gives us an entirely new perspective on everything.

A particular path, while purposeful in the beginning, is but a stepping-stone. Pathways often simply drop away once we awaken, feeling rather heavy, burdensome, and superfluous. We might liken the different paths to a planned car trip from Dallas to Chicago, with many stops along the way. Once we arrive in Chicago, our final destination, the route is no longer needed or even thought about much, but discarded with gratitude that its job is done. This doesn't mean we may not still enjoy aspects of a path we once loved, but it's no longer "our path," which is a big difference.

Embrace the Paradoxes of Relative Versus Absolute Truth

The reason there are so many paths is that the human

expression of our essential being is privy to relative truth, while the soul remains always connected to absolute truth. It's the blending of the two that affords us understanding of the larger perspective of oneness that holds all relative reality in place—a reality that's real to the senses but isn't absolute reality.

Many become caught in the snares of relative truth and fail to see the possibility that more than one perspective can be valid at the same time. They then imagine they alone are on the "right" path. However, relative truth and absolute truth aren't at odds with one another—it's all a matter of perspective.

One of the problems our planet faces is people's limited perspectives. Many of the world's ills can be traced to people believing their understanding is the correct one, which has led them to engage in witch burnings, pogroms, crusades, suicide bombings, and mass terrorism, not to mention countless daily struggles.

Beginning to awaken has taught me that the only thing anyone might know in terms of absolute truth is that the journey is a mystery beyond comprehension. I know nothing for sure other than what my current vantage point tells me. In fact, I no longer wish to read any book or listen to any teacher who claims otherwise. Life simply isn't cut-and-dried. It is for this reason that this book focuses on *my* awakening journey rather than on the one and only awakening journey. I wouldn't want it any other way.

Paradoxes abound in the relative universe. For example, death and no-death are both true for a person who blends relative and absolute truth. Likewise, right and wrong—and even no right and wrong—are both true for such a person. What can appear as opposites from our physical perspective coexist purposefully and peacefully from the broader perspective of soul, allowing us to acknowledge them together. Peace comes from seeing both relative and absolute truth, then resting either in the middle or, in some cases, in the not knowing. Learning to rest within the paradoxes of relative and absolute truth is an important step in the awakening process.

The whole of reality exists in the oneness. We can be spiritual or not, and we are in the oneness. We can run ten miles each morning or sleep until noon, and we are in the oneness. We can be a "pious" priest or a "naughty" stripper, and we are in the oneness. We can live a life of total virtue or a life of crime, and we are still in the oneness. It may surprise you to hear that each of these paths can lead to awakening just as easily as any other.

Where Is Your Path Taking You?

Since all paths, when followed too rigidly, create a huge barrier to awakening, how are we to know when a path is no longer right for us? The deciding factor in whether it serves us or hinders us is whether it leads us to walk through the largest doorway within, which is that of soul.

In my own journey, as I continued to go deeper and closer in, becoming more intimate with my own soul, it became clear to me that all the different pathways are simply a means to an *interior* destination that's *complete in itself*. I'm speaking of an inner awakening that enables us to *live* oneness, and therefore wholeness, as an experienced reality rather than as an intellectual ideal that, in this life, is usually only attained by select saints and gurus.

In my experience, the shift from role to soul can be much more clear and direct if we don't become lost on distinct paths for years and years. To avoid getting lost, as so many are, it's crucial to understand that the various paths are all simply a means to arriving at *no path*, which is what I mean when I speak of enlightenment, awakening, or the experience of oneness. If we can get from role to soul, we no longer need outside belief systems and their accompanying practices and support groups to sustain us, since we sustain *ourselves*.

We take a huge leap forward once we recognize that the various paths are only matters of personal preference. There's only the path *inward*, which ultimately leads to no path at all. We come to a point where living from soul feels the most whole, the most like home. It's then that we know deep in our bones there are no outer paths to take us where we really desire to go.

The important thing is to *find our own way*. How we choose to put our "pieces" together is up to us—and *only* us. There are endless approaches, and each of us needs to be guided solely by our own soul. To imagine someone else "has it together" in a way that we can only aspire to only delays our own awakening. If there are any fully awakened beings walking among us, and I believe there may well be, there's a good chance they aren't among those trying to enlighten us! In all likelihood they live in relative obscurity and aren't on what's known as the spirituality circuit.

The teacher and the student live deep inside each one of us. There's not *necessarily* much to teach. There's not *necessarily* much to learn. Although we can certainly help one another along the way, ultimately we come to see that there's only a shift in perspective to be made. *From Role to Soul* is a simple reflection on what this shift in perspective has looked and felt like *for me* as I came to remember the real me.

In my own life, I found there's a time for a path and a time for no path, and the shifts on my awakening journey expressed in this book lead to the latter as a "final" inner destination, which is about living as simply myself, day to day, moment by moment, soul to soul.

It took me decades to comprehend that my own inner truth is really the only path— and, ultimately, not a path at all. Instead, it's me being a willing vehicle for the expression of the oneness. That's it. That's all.

PART 1

3

Living Free

Several years ago I had the most interesting dream in which my mouth acted as a huge magnet drawing from within me different kinds of metal pins, nails, needles, and screws—all of them a variety of shapes, sizes, and degrees of sharpness. They were coming from every nook and cranny of my body. It was uncomfortable, yet at the same time felt like a necessity—and a relief. My mouth continued to fill and fill with sharp objects, pricking the soft folds without piercing them. When I couldn't hold a single piece more, I opened my mouth wider than I could have ever imagined, whereupon all of the pins, nails, needles, and screws began gently floating out and away. I was surprised how readily and easily they left me. The process of clearing the metal out continued for a long while. With each release, I felt both gratitude and relief. After the experience was over I was exhausted, yet strangely content. I awoke at 5 a.m. feeling as if I had been spring cleaned internally. The dream has never left me.

Because this dream had that rare texture of realness, aliveness, and value that few dreams exhibit, I actually awakened my husband to share. As we discussed it, I described it as similar to scenes in the movie The Green

Mile, in which Michael Clarke Duncan's character heals others by sucking out toxicity that's causing illness in their bodies, then releasing what appear to be little buzzing flies that dissipate into the air.

To me, my dream was a metaphor for the process of dismantling my ego. As we move deeper into living from soul, we discover there's paradoxically both less and more of who we know ourselves to be. Less of all that our ego thinks is real, including much of the ruckus on the different paths, and at the same time more spaciousness than we have ever known. Oneness is both vast and singular. The more we integrate this truth, the more aware we become that the awakening journey is actually one of *shedding*, not *adding*.

When I speak of shedding ego, I ought to explain that "ego" is a term that has been used in different ways in different eras and by different disciplines, such as philosophy, psychology, and spirituality. Depending on the context in which it appears, it can mean anything from our true self, to our estimation of ourselves in the sense of how we judge our worth, to a totally false sense of ourselves. By "ego," *I* mean all of the ways we identify ourselves that keep us from knowing our true self as simply soul embodied as human. It's the images and ideas we hold of ourselves and carry around in our head. When our life is based on ego, sadly we aren't very conscious. Instead, it's like we are walking around in a daze.

Let me also be clear what I mean by "conscious." The quality I'm referring to has to do with how *aware* we are. Have you ever noticed that people have different levels of awareness? Walking down a city street, some of us notice all kinds of details about the stores, the shoppers, the traffic, whereas others honestly can't remember walking past a particular shop or group of people.

Similarly, in a conversation or listening to a lecture, some of us catch the drift of what's being said much more readily than others. We can also recall more of what was said because we were, well, more "present." Our minds weren't elsewhere.

People are aware—conscious—to different degrees. In no area of life is this more the case than when it comes to truly "knowing" our own self. We just aren't aware of the things we say, even some of the things we do, much of the time. Even less are we aware of why we do many of the things we do, meaning our motives. Taking it a step further, how many of us are aware of whether we are truly doing what we want to do? How many of us are in touch with what actually makes us "tick"?

The dream about the metal objects in my mouth occurred at a time when I was becoming aware and beginning to consciously make the shift from role to soul. I was learning that many of the images I had of myself in particular roles, mostly borrowed from others, were keeping me from knowing and living a life based on all that's true and real about me. The dream signified for me the beginning stages of an emotional untethering from those aspects of my life that pushed my energies into creating and maintaining my various personas—those aspects of myself I presented to the world as my "personality," or what I call the ego.

Behind every possible external label, and beyond every possible outer identification, is our soul. We must begin to think of ourselves, feel ourselves, and know ourselves as soul. This is our primary state—who we are.

The Soul Behind the Role

After years of metaphysical and spiritual study, I finally took my first conscious step towards the shift from role to soul as a *lived* reality. Such a shift is imperative for anyone who is on a journey of awakening to who they truly are. This shift requires us to enter into a process that

I will dub "unforgetting." We have to learn to recall what we have forgotten, which is that we are each really a soul wearing different suits of clothing, which are the roles we fulfill. Through this "unforgetting," we come to see that much human suffering stems from *not remembering* that we are soul rather than role.

From our earliest days, the push by well-meaning others is to know the universe by looking outward, always outward. But one of the paradoxes of life is that the universe can only truly be known by looking inward. It's because we look outward that we identify with our different roles instead of primarily with soul. This misidentification entrenches us in relative truths, locking us into a limited, narrow perspective of reality that leaves little room to perceive the ultimate nature of our being. None of us is the person we label ourselves as. Instead, we exist permanently and forevermore beyond and behind all of the parameters we create for ourselves. When we attach to labels, narrow scopes, and rigid perspectives, we slowly but surely give away our power to an external source. To awaken, we must look inward to soul, which allows us to release the continual need to label and defend our roles.

We can't know our soul if we see ourselves only in terms of human roles. To illustrate, suppose you identify yourself as a runner. "I'm a runner," you tell yourself. Then you have an injury that puts a permanent end to your running, as happened to a friend of mine. Who are you now? From the perspective of your role as a runner, you've experienced a huge loss. An entire persona has simply vanished overnight. But from the perspective of soul, you are still you.

We could multiply such examples almost endlessly. For instance, if you are expecting, you may have begun to identify yourself as a mother. Perhaps you've bought all kinds of things to help you fulfill this role, such as a crib, feeding bottles, baby clothes. Maybe you redecorated one of the rooms in your house. You might even have chosen to quit your job. But what happens to the role of mother if your baby is tragically born dead or dies shortly after birth?

How many people who have been made redundant, or forced to take early retirement, feel utterly lost when they no longer have a role in the labor force? Their days seem endless, their lives empty, because all they have known themselves to be was their role on the job.

I've seen how this works in practice in my own family. Not long ago, within a span of six months, my son broke his wrist on the first day of his beloved travel baseball season and ended up missing the entire season, while my daughter tore her labrum and eventually needed surgery during her high school tennis season. There was quite a difference in how the injuries were perceived by all involved—the child, the parents, and others.

In our son's case, the injury felt much more devastating because he's so strongly identified with being an athlete, and specifically a baseball player. We went through a painful process of breaking down the role he holds onto so tightly. The point was for him to see that while athleticism is a beautiful box and a gift to be appreciated, he's so much more than that box.

In our older daughter's case, the roles are less defined. She doesn't identify herself with specific roles quite so much, and neither do others think of her in terms of roles. Her self-understanding is more organic, more whole. Her injury and subsequent surgery felt much more like simply a new experience to explore than a big loss.

To be able to say "I am," without adding other words to this statement, comes more easily for our daughter than for our son. To witness these two injuries side by side, and become aware of our different perceptions of each, was an eye-opener in terms of the shift from role to soul—not only with regard to how we see ourselves, but also how we view others.

When external circumstances force us to abandon a role, which they often do, it becomes less painful, and eventually of little consequence, once we know the freedom of living from soul instead of role. A role is akin to a character in a drama. When we're done with playing our dramatic part, we might become a character in a comedy. The two are quite different, but what hasn't changed is who *we* are as the actor playing the parts—the soul behind the role.

Insight from a Movie

After watching the movie Milk, about the famous activist Harvey Milk who was the first gay person to be elected to public office in California, it occurred to me that we *all* have closets to come out of. Countless closets, in fact. For when we emerge from one, we find there's another and another and another, perhaps all of a different stripe, but closets just the same. We are all imprisoned in our own closets, the ego states attached to the roles behind which we hide from ourselves.

Have you ever considered that all of the different roles, labels, and identifications you are enmeshed in prevent you from being whole? They are merely weak impersonations of the real deal. Just beneath them is wholeness.

This movie made me wonder what it would be like to get completely soul naked. I'm talking about no longer navigating life from a place of hiding within a closet of my own making, but instead navigating in full view from soul. As I started to try this out, I realized that if we consciously went everywhere *as soul*, we would know *wholeness*.

To stay with the case of Harvey Milk, it may seem that coming out of the closet solidified his identification with the role of gay male. Paradoxically, such a move is actually a shift towards wholeness and truth. When we let go of our identification of ourselves with ego to the point that we become soul naked, we discover that no identification of *any* kind is needed. We can just be the person we find ourselves to be.

In the days when I was caught up in my personas and the roles attached to them, I tried to serve through my various roles. As sincere as I was, I often missed what others truly needed from me. This was because, when we know ourselves primarily by our roles, we are in our various closets, each of which represents one of our fractured parts. Viewing others from these closets, we can't help but see them in the light of a projection of our own fragmentation. The consequence is that we aren't able to connect with them authentically, which means we not only experience ourselves as largely separate from others but much of the time are unaware of what it takes to be of meaningful service.

If we can stop investing our time and energy in our roles as if they were our identity, we can allow ourselves to know our soul, which is whole. The shift from role to soul changes everything, leading us to an entirely new way of seeing and being within the same life—*our* precious life.

Awakening is ultimately only about reaching core truth. The movement is basically from "I am (fill in the blank)," to simply, "I Am." Fully embracing "I Am" becomes the primary truth from which all else in our life flows. Everything added to this statement brings the complexity associated with ego rather than soul simplicity. The key is to live no longer tethered to all of the many identities that could accompany the "I am" statement, and instead live fully embodied as the soul that's our true identity.

How to Live in a Way that Makes a Difference

As we shed our attachment to roles as our identity—as we move away from the various personas of the ego—we begin to feel a deep connection with everyone and everything, which engenders love and a longing to make a difference. I find that, the more I awaken to my own being, what I really desire when it comes to others is soul communion—a simple capacity to enjoy one another—as we both agree to *come as we are*.

What a world this would be if everyone were to simply "come as they are." It's when we experience self-transformation through awakening more and more of our being that we are at last *truly* able to come as we are, which is when we begin to make a real difference in the world if this is what our soul desires.

As Lao-Tzu explained two and a half millennia ago, "Would you really like to save the world from the degradation and destruction it seems destined for? Then step away from shallow mass movements and quietly go work on your own self-awareness. If you want to awaken all of humanity, awaken all of yourself. If you want to eliminate the suffering in the world, then eliminate all that is dark and negative in yourself. Truly the greatest gift you have to give is that of your own self-transformation."

Lao Tzu is pointing to the remarkable shift that happens as we focus on our own self-transformation instead of on changing the exterior world. Paradoxically, the more we eliminate all that's dark and negative in ourselves, the more we find ourselves making a difference in the lives of others. The reason for this is that out of this holistic state, an intense love for humanity develops, generating a desire to engage in selfless service—ways of making a difference in the world based not on our own neediness and the projections that originate from this neediness, but on our emerging wholeness.

As we increasingly become joyfully grounded in our physical bodies, and extremely grateful to be so, we simultaneously come to view the world from both a state of high self-love and oneness. This blended perspective is now at the forefront of our awareness, informing all thoughts, priorities, activities, and choices. Imagine if this were the way heads of state approached international negotiations, how CEOs steered their companies, and how management and labor interacted!

Having said this, it would be a complete fantasy to imagine that shifting is only about love, compassion, and bliss. Awakening is about truth, which can be a confrontational, uncomfortable, and frequently messy process. Since ultimately we are solely responsible for our own personal growth, self-confrontation grounded in self-examination is the most effective and least painful way of moving toward becoming whole adults.

Coming from a fulfilled, increasingly integrated state, a level of high service from the soul becomes possible right alongside some of the messy aspects of our development. Much that's unessential is now shed. Life lived simply, and simply lived, becomes more than enough—as we understand that *we* are enough, and the burden of the proof of self-worth falls away. So by focusing on our own self-transformation instead of on fixing the world around us, our egoic need to feel validated evaporates, leaving us free to pour ourselves into truly worthwhile self-expression. In short, as we take the inner journey, we increasingly self-realize in creative external ways.

This phase of awakening, in which the ego almost completely falls away, is what many refer to as living in non-duality. In place of ego, our true being is now accessed. Individuation is experienced and lived through the unified lens of oneness—a wonderful blending. The veil between personal and impersonal has become very thin. Life as we knew it no longer appears at all the same from the inside looking out, although it might look exactly the same from the outside looking in.

This more developed aspect of awakening is still quite rare. Many masters who have written about a state they refer to as "no self" are often pointing to this aspect of awakening, in which the ego essentially disappears so that oneness may be experienced and lived.

By "no self," what the masters are referring to is no ego—no image we carry around in our head of ourselves in our various roles. In a sense, we don't *think* of ourselves at all because we are too engaged in simply *being* ourselves. For the person who is totally aware, all self-consciousness disappears. As more and more enter into this awareness of themselves as an expression of the oneness that's the source of everyone and everything, it will lift humanity and the planet to new heights.

PART 1

4

The Shifts

As we journey, we eventually come to know who we truly *are*—and simultaneously come to know, and let go of, who we truly *are not*. The shifts facilitate both these phases of our development—getting to know and own who we are, while simultaneously letting go of who we aren't. There isn't much more to it than that. Consequently the awakening journey is as much about moving *away from* as it is about moving toward.

Keep in mind that not only what we are shifting to, but also what we are shifting from, exists in the oneness. So it's not really about forsaking the *from* to embrace the *to*, but rather we simply become much more aware of and available to the *to*, which is typically a more expansive vantage point.

Awakening allows us to experience every day from the perspective of oneness in which the human manifestation of our soul is cherished and celebrated. When we can blend with ease the sacrilegious and the sublime, the profane and the profound, the blasphemous and the sacred, the pain and the joy, we will be able to accept not only ourselves fully, but also to accept each and every person whatever their particular path. With such acceptance, we truly know everyday oneness on this plane.

Let me be clear what I mean by "accept." I'm not talking about merely putting up with a situation; I'm referring to being able to embrace it. To illustrate, an awakened therapist once asked a friend who was suffering the acute pain of a kidney stone, "Did you give thanks for your kidney stone this morning?" Do you hear the non-duality in this? When we embrace *all* of reality, it's no longer simply *There's much suffering in life* (our physicality), but also *All is Well* (soul). It feels as if the joy of being a soul exists above, below, and within the human predicament. And indeed it does, for they share the same space. This is peace in the paradox.

Such paradoxes are prevalent in life, so expect to encounter them in every nook and cranny of your journey. I suggest we all get used to them and embrace them. Personally, I look for them in all my experiences. In fact, I relish them for what they have to teach me about how to live more deeply. I've learned that everything that happens in life is a tool to bring us to the felt experience of oneness, which can be "known" and yet is impossible to describe.

Painful experiences we might be tempted to run from are part of the oneness, which is why awakening for many people is triggered by a catalyst such as a crisis, an illness, a significant loss, or some other event. However, it's also true that awakening can spring from a shift in our intellectual understanding—which can also rock our world—and then all of the other shifts that may not be accentuated during this time are given a gateway to emerge. If allowed to, the many shifts we experience on the journey of awakening begin to occur organically as we embody them from inside out.

Fifteen Shifts

In the second part of *From Role to Soul,* I outline fifteen shifts that are meant to be guideposts in the sense of reference points for people at different places on the awakening journey. The shifts I allude to don't provide in-depth information on each topic, but instead offer a personal reflection on how a shift may look and feel—a sort of "what to expect." They are also a "keep developing" confirmation. And for those who appreciate a good mirror, they are a way to compare notes.

You'll be encouraged by my relating of how some of the shifts took me a lot longer to integrate than others, so they feel more hard-won. Around those shifts I simply had more hidden shadows, life themes, and core wounds to illuminate. It will be the same for you, albeit surrounding different shifts.

It's important to realize we are each coming from a point of distinct past conditioning. For example, if you are a mother, as I am, my mother complex may have manifested much differently from yours, and therefore how my awakening occurred will be different from your experience of awakening. But while the front-end of the shifts may appear different for each person, the end result—the expanded perspective gained from each shift—will be similar, since the overall awakening journey is a universal one. For this reason, we must trust that all others are quite capable of growth from their own life situations.

Writing this book has helped me to know myself better. But the most important thing about my offering it to the public is for you, the reader, to make these shifts about *you*. How they relate to *your* inner truth and experiences is really the only issue. The shifts that occurred for me may or may not occur for you, and yet they will each provide you with insight—either because you resonate with them, or perchance because you don't. Either way you'll learn something about yourself.

One reason you may not resonate with some of the shifts I experienced is that I'm not equipped to write about anyone else's awakening. Some may have a radical awakening that typically occurs after a dark night of the soul. Mine, while it's true that I experienced many dark nights of different textures, has been a gradual shift in perspective that has accelerated and become more sustainable over time through darker nights as well as lighter ones.

My awakening had absolutely nothing to do with hierarchies, formalities, or rules. On the contrary, it had everything to do with paying attention to the ordinary within a life simply lived, free of "much ado about nothing." In the end, I found that even once-cherished practices were no longer necessary, as awareness became the norm rather than the rarity. It has been a deeply personal journey, with nothing else needed other than my willingness and desire to become more intimate with my soul as it expresses itself in the form of my humanness—a blending of my inner and outer worlds. It has been an awakening by degrees, with my own life as the only barometer.

The fifteen shifts I describe bring awareness of ourselves as soul fully into the material realm, so that soul is no longer compartmentalized as if it were separate from who we are and how we live. The shifts are definitely *not* meant to elicit a feeling of cut and dried, black and white, and either-or. For me, most of the shifts feel like a movement from primary focus to secondary focus—or the opposite, however you choose to look at it.

Each Person's Path Is Unique

After a while it began to be evident to me that the various aspects of awakening *choose us,* and we in turn must then choose to participate. This is why there can never be a "system" for awakening—and also why the shifts

I describe that brought about my own awakening are in no particular order. They all occurred for me over more than two decades, and in an overlapping, circular, and often simultaneous way. Since our individual circumstances are unique, and since soul uses our circumstances to awaken us, the aspect of each shift we are focusing on at a particular time will be specific to us.

I learned that sometimes shifts take place unconsciously—although I've found them to be much more delicious when experienced fully self-aware, so that we actually feel them emerging from soul, filling both heart and mind as they do so. Hence one of the keys to moving forward is to actively choose the awakening experiences that choose us, which means really going with them. When a shift begins, what's required is our response in each and every moment, so that our development becomes an interplay between what life asks of us at any given instant and how we respond.

I find that the different circumstances of our lives are constantly reaching out to stimulate our capacity for growth, seeking to dismantle ego, draw out our authentic being, and immerse us in awareness of oneness. It's an ongoing process, so that the next step is likely just around the corner. The shifts are so intimately connected with our unique makeup and life situation that they rise and fall into our consciousness over and over in new ways, with each fresh uncovering stemming from our own lived life. The shifts are all still occurring for me as they deepen into the wholeness that is Annie.

In the end, each of the fifteen shifts I cover in *From Role to Soul* add up to wholeness and thereby return us to the oneness that exists within the inner flame known as our soul. Eventually, our total willingness to simply show up as a conscious, individuated vehicle of and for oneness propels our awakening without us having to do or be anything other than what we naturally are.

The Transformative Power of Watching Ourselves

I mentioned that my awakening involved paying greater attention to the ordinary within a life simply lived. I have found that a powerful practice to help us make the shifts required to move from role to soul is to observe ourselves playing the various characters we play the part of in everyday life. All we need to do is watch ourselves in our roles, conducting check-ins with ourselves so that we begin to see the different costumes we employ to cover our soul.

To start watching ourselves in our various roles—to witness ourselves as the star we are of our very own play—can seem surreal at first. But as the process of uncovering our essential being gets underway, it's actually exciting to begin "unidentifying" with the characters and costumes, until we come to know who we are *behind* those roles we project outward into the world. With practice paying attention, we slowly become an impartial observer of our own ego states. As we do so, we begin moving more fully into an awareness of ourselves as what I refer to as a "blended" being. As ego is stripped away and we stop thinking of ourselves in prescribed ways, we discover that we are fully a part of the ultimate oneness and yet unique individual expressions of this oneness.

The top layers of our ego are seen with fairly easy clarity. These aspects of our self-image pertain to our roles as parent, spouse, sister, friend, teacher, musician. If we choose to go even further into the awakening process, we begin to peer closely at the more deeply embedded layers of our character. These include labels involving such aspects of our everyday life as our ethnicity, nationality, gender, and sexuality.

We are so used to witnessing ourselves from a segregated vantage point that to see ourselves in an integrated way can at first be challenging. Despite this, the shift from segregated to integrated is a crucial part of the awakening journey. It's for this reason that an ongoing process of self-examination is helpful. We become a witness to our own ego at work through our thoughts, emotions, and choices, day in and day out. Simultaneously, we can train ourselves to look at ourselves in a manner that encompasses our wholeness, rather than identifying with our different parts, personas, and projects. By so doing, we learn to feel the difference between the voices of role and the voice of soul.

Seeing how we closet ourselves off in the ego states connected with our roles— witnessing ourselves "in character"—is an important step in the sometimes difficult inner work of dismantling the ego to arrive at simply soul. I found that a gradual simplification of my ego-driven life allowed for a deeper friendship with my soul. As I gradually made the shift from role to soul, I began to feel the beauty of all that I am.

As my self-awareness grew, I also became empowered to make choices that cultivated an ease as I moved through my different roles, so that life increasingly flowed as I took on a role and set it down.

I also found that because I was more aware, I could choose *not* to closet myself by identifying myself in some limited way as I declared, "This is who I am." Likewise I learned to stop limiting myself by thinking twice before I said of something life was asking of me, "That's not me."

From role to soul changes everything we thought we knew about who we are. It's so much more than the word "shift" can convey, so much more than a mere cerebral expansion. Paradoxically, it turns out that although we are moving into our soul, it's a far more effective way to navigate our humanness. Coming from soul, a wholeness permeates our lives—a wholeness we in turn offer the world. As the unifying state of oneness grows gradually within us, we come to know our own divine core and are therefore able to recognize the divine core in all others, since they are connected to us in the oneness. It's realizing this commonality that awakens us to compassion, whereby service begins to flourish and eventually abound.

PART 2

15 Shifts to "Awakening"

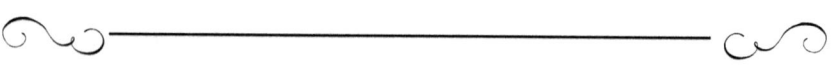

SHIFT

#1

From Role to Soul

From Identification to Wholeness
From Ego to Soul
From Personality to Core
From False-Self to True-Self
From Character to Actor

The spiritual journey does not consist of arriving at a new destination where a person gains what he did not have, or becomes what he is not. It consists in the dissipation of one's own ignorance concerning oneself and life, and the gradual growth of that understanding which begins the spiritual awakening.
Aldous Huxley

Recently I have been thinking a lot about life and death, but mainly life. The truth is, no matter how much we may resist the notion, we are all terminal. And if we really let this sink in, really contemplate it for more than a few seconds, allowing it to become not a morbid aspect of our existence but a reminder to live truly and to truly live, we may find ourselves wanting to at least consider some changes in our lives.

Always a walker, I have enjoyed especially long walks during the more recent part of my journey and almost feel like a shepherd—the walking part, not the herding part. As I walk, I contemplate how my life has become streamlined during the past few years, so that it's fairly simple, gentle, and peaceful. After decades on a self-exploratory path, I've come to the realization that, for the most part, I'm living the life I would wish to be living were I to be told that I had only a short time left. On these long walks, I've carefully reviewed the different choices made on a regular basis that allow this to be so.

While I realize we're all wired differently and must live within our particular means and circumstances, I believe we can each create an external life that mirrors as closely as possible our inner life, often much more so than we might realize. In the western world many of us have our basic needs met more than adequately compared with most of the people on our planet. Once these needs are met, priorities are ours to set, choices ours to make. It's in this way that the shift I speak of occurs—priority by priority, choice by choice. Even if our situation is a difficult one, we can still make choices that more closely reflect a recognition of what in this precious life *we* deem most important.

The shift from role to soul empowers us to navigate life from a wider perspective than is ordinarily perceived as living in the "real world." Approaching life from this vantage point, I find I don't draw lines in the sand for myself. I've become more of a *for me, for now* kinda gal, always open to the next moment, the next day, the next soul-to-soul encounter.

When we come from this broader outlook, our definitions of "successful," "normal," and "productive" may not match those of the mainstream. In my own life, fitting in with the norm has in so many ways fallen by the wayside as I've become much more in touch with soul.

How Awakening Changed Me

To illustrate the changes that may come about as we awaken, let me share some of my own experiences. Yours will be different, perhaps even the opposite of mine in some cases. As you'll see, I became less busy, whereas you may choose to become busier. Whatever the specific issue, my point is that the changes we make as we awaken enable us to approach life from soul rather than role.

I'll begin with how exercise has changed for me. After years of taking exercise classes, or at least feeling I "should" be in them, I came to the realization that, generally speaking, I most enjoy exercising alone, outside in the different seasons, and in ways that feed my soul as much as my body. Although walking, biking, and swimming may not create a fierce outer buff, I realize that my priority is inner buff. If swimming the breast stroke and dolphin diving result in greater external buff, I regard it as icing on the cake.

My financial status is another area in which soul has come to dominate role. For years I strove to make a "name" for myself. I wanted to make it "big," which of course is the American dream. But even though I was engaged in work that fed my soul and was fully integrated with my own personal development, my feelings about work are now much more in alignment with the slower-paced, non-hectic life I truly desire. Could I be making more money? For sure. Could our family upgrade our residence to a house with more than three bedrooms and a single upstairs family bathroom? We could certainly make this a priority. Could I work harder? Yes—and yet I don't really want to. Instead, I desire to enjoy the blessed life I already have.

Socially, my husband and I always stayed in the loop, accepting countless invitations to events over the course of several years. Yet today, by mutual choice, we've virtually dropped out of the social scene in our area. We came to realize that although we're both outgoing, giving, friendly individuals who like all kinds of people and certainly enjoy a good time, the large parties, philanthropic events, and planned-in-advance dinner outings we used to engage in aren't truly our thing. We much prefer spontaneous, more intimate gatherings, and our current social life reflects this.

I also got out of the rat race of believing I always needed to be "busy." You know what I mean—running lots of errands like so many other moms with whom I interact (and dads, too). I now find I have few errands to run, which is liberating. A minimalist at heart, getting rid of things rather than accumulating more has become a priority, at least to the degree that being a family of five permits.

I also felt I should be multitasking, as if it were a badge of honor for a modern mother—until the day I awakened to the fact that I'm much more effective when I'm task-specific. So these days I perform a task, then discover there's plenty of space to simply "be" until the need arises to engage in another undertaking. All of the "busyness" people talk about—the feeling that one rarely has time to sit down—is simply no longer my reality. I realize that some thrive on being busy; but I'm not one of them, preferring a much simpler existence.

I used to think a lot about food in terms of what was good or not good for my health and weight. Today I'm far less rule-bound, preferring to listen to my body and eat a balance of foods. There are definitely splurges here and there. There are lighter eating days and heavier eating days. I incorporate a thoughtful balance of proteins and carbs. Generally speaking though, I'm not out to be anything other than who I am. I don't desire a life in which I can't enjoy food, even if it means a less sculpted body than I could attain through restrictive eating habits and a more rigid exercise regime.

For quite a few years I regularly attended lectures and workshops. Now I rarely involve myself in any of these. When the opportunity to attend an event is brought to my attention, I listen to my heart, which always tells me either "partake" or "pass." It's become as simple and as clear as that, even for those events others perceive as mandatory.

Another way in which I've become much more in touch with soul and less engaged in role is my family. I realize that the years in the nest as an immediate family are fleeting. Everyday moments of togetherness enjoyed in one another's presence pass quickly. It's so important to live *true* to oneself in each of these moments, which is the only way they can be both meaningful and memorable. As a side benefit, we also handle the challenges of family life more effectively when we come from authenticity, since being authentic is a wellspring of fortitude and strength.

Living more from soul than role is a great way of living—and dying. It's about living *like* we are dying. As a fellow blogger put it, are we writing a *eulogy* or a *resume*?

On my quiet walks, one theme comes up again and again with total knowing. I know in my heart of hearts and deep in my bones that, upon my actual death, my one and only certain regret would be if I had lived my life according to someone else's definitions of "successful," "normal," and "productive."

Don't Fence Me In, Baby!

For many years now my husband and I have raised our children to know themselves simply as soul expressed in human form. However, since we were both raised to identify ourselves as Christians, we still adhere to some of the Christian traditions. On a recent Easter Sunday, while relating the story of Jesus to our children as we always do during this season, my husband and I laughed as it struck us that we could also identify ourselves in that moment as being Jewish. Something about this particular break with traditional thinking enabled us to see we have no need to identify ourselves as *any* one thing, and that to do so limits our ability to be fully ourselves, truly whole. We both experienced a strong feeling of *Don't Fence Us In*. We are so much more than any particular role, any specific identity.

Our ego identifications can be a heavy load to carry, so that there comes a time when the gratification from the roles becomes less and the burden more. As the shift from role to soul percolated inside me, in due course it became apparent I no longer had a desire to identify myself in singular ways. It was then I discovered that if enough of our roles are set aside, reserved for times of practicality, we are left to live fully from our soul. As we begin tending our inner garden, we bloom from the inside out. To live this way is freeing and exciting—so different from the way many of us are mesmerized by external pursuits.

I perform the roles of woman, mother, wife, teacher, author, friend, daughter, speaker, lawn mower, laundress, soul nurturer, planner, nature lover, blogger, walker, neighbor, biker, reader, and so many more. Such roles are all associated with what I *do*, but are only temporary expressions of who I *am*. I wear labels that brand me as spiritual, liberal, Caucasian, holistic, kind, healthy, feminine, Midwestern, American, heterosexual, middle-aged, introspective, and on and on. I realize I'm ultimately none of these. Any one of them could change at any moment, even disappear from my life, and yet I would remain the same.

Were I to lose my ability to walk, I may no longer be a walker, but I would still be me. Were I to lose my capacity to teach, I may no longer be a teacher, but I would still be me. Were my marriage to end, I may no longer be a wife, but I would still be me. I would still be me quite apart from every single one of my many ways of identifying myself. It's this "me" behind all of these labels that has the capacity for true soul-to-soul connection with you. It's this "me" that lies beyond all that my personality appears to be, that has the capacity to know the exquisite truth of our oneness.

The more I recognize myself as an expression of ultimate oneness, the more I experience what it is to know myself as soul rather than role, and the less I need labels to define me. So much so that there came a point when, despite being on what I referred to as a spiritual journey for years, calling the missing piece a "spiritual" piece began to feel too confining. In the end it came to feel like just more separation, more layers, whereas the truth is that everything is in the oneness, and the oneness is in everything. I came to feel rather fenced in and somewhat trapped by any form of external identification.

As you contemplate the different ways you define yourself, you too may discover that your roles are holding at bay a greater intimacy with the only part of you that's ultimately real. Labels keep us from living authentically from moment to moment, day to day, and soul to soul, imprisoning us in personal expectations that are often nothing more than societal norms having nothing to do with who we are in the truest sense.

Although at times the roles may be convenient for practical purposes, they typically block out the most important aspects of relationships and interactions—the warmth, the space, and the love that naturally emanate from what lies underneath. As I'm learning not to fence myself in, I encourage you not to fence yourself in—and not to fence others in either. Because we are all so much more than our roles, we can choose to live beyond the roles. We offer the highest to ourselves, as well as to each other, when we see clearly what we truly are—soul.

FROM ROLE TO SOUL

While it doesn't happen overnight that we come to focus less on role and more on soul, gradually we get to know our Big Me, the "I Am" at the core of our being. Because it isn't a persona, isn't limited, and isn't incomplete, it encompasses everything and denies nothing. There are no delineations. It rises *into* the doing involved in all our roles. From this vantage, it becomes much easier to fathom the Big We. And from there, it's possible to uplift the whole world.

I'm learning to shift my focus away from all the qualities that make up the "little me," choosing instead to go forth in full recognition and appreciation of the Big Me and the Big You that make up the Big We, which is eternally connected to the source of all things, the universal oneness.

Facebook—My Daughters, Me, and an Unexpected Gift

My two teenage daughters and I, like most mothers and daughters, share much within the daily familial spectrum. For us, due to an openness and a conscious desire to *see* each other full-on in all of our giddy, emotional glory, our relationship is so much more than the parent-child role. It truly is soul to soul.

Surprisingly, Facebook—yes, Facebook, a medium I resisted during its initial phases—has created the historically *rare* opportunity for my daughters to see their mother be herself, joyfully self-express, interact with numerous others, muse via different forms of writing, and generally shine unapologetically to the world at large.

I discussed this recent epiphany with my older daughter just this week as it dawned on me that I never knew my mom as much more than my mom while I was growing up. Sure, she had a tremendous influence on me as the beautiful woman she continues to be, and fortunately we've now come to know each other's insides better. Still, I've never really seen her up close and personal with the world, offering her insights, life lessons, and individual truths. I know I would have appreciated her in a broader sense at a much younger age had there been more opportunities for her to self-express, share, and flourish. I would have loved to *see* and *feel* more of her soul. I wish that I had known long ago what she loved, so that I had a means of connecting to her soul.

Not that this is the only way to go in a parent-child simpatico, since this relationship is such a unique and intimate one for each of us. But it struck me strongly, in the form of a deep feeling of gratitude, that my two daughters are seeing a sermon in *action* rather than hearing one. It made me smile to think that after many years of *hiding my light under a bushel* due to psychic debris, today, as I uncage my soul publicly, my very own dear, dear daughters have front row seats. For even though they tease me about commenting too much and being a thumbs-up fanatic, I can see in their eyes that I'm giving them permission to be themselves and live true.

If it weren't for Facebook, my work as a soul nurturer and writer, which is intertwined with my own personal growth in many ways, would remain largely hidden from my family, other than something discussed at the dinner table. They aren't present at my talks, Soul to Soul Circles, or private sessions, and yet because of Facebook they see me (often and sometimes *too* much) beyond the typical mom role. While I love my mom role, to view a parent from different vantage points can be beneficial to children, especially as they reach adolescence. The enlarged aerial view acts as a mirror for them to see *their* potential as a multifaceted being. My grandest desire for all three of my children is that they enjoy being a blended being and appreciate the sacredness of *all* aspects of the journey.

Whether it be navigating their own emotional landscape in a conscious, fearless way, pursuing a career that matches their individual interior longings, or creating transparent, loving relationships, I want my children to live from their soul. We can't teach another how to do this through mere words. We must become capable of living it ourselves. For my children to feel comfortable in their own skin, both privately and publicly, has always been a high priority in my parenting.

While it hasn't been easy understanding and coming to terms with my own fears and psychic debris, I decided with joy and certainty that I was willing to go first. Increasingly liberating myself to be fully me is my greatest accomplishment as both an individual and a parent. The self-love that begins to flourish on this path of deeper self-awareness has many ripple effects. With every step we take as parents to free ourselves from living behind masks, we invite our beloved children to do the same.

Wholeness cannot be underestimated as a path to both personal and worldwide peace. Today I feel grateful to Facebook for unknowingly and unexpectedly giving me a vehicle not only to share my "Annieness" with friends far and wide, but most importantly with my beautiful teenage daughters who are observing me carefully to understand what it means to be an embodied soul. I hope my willingness to "come out" as both the silly and deep soul I am paves the way for my children to come out as simply themselves too.

Listening to Van Morrison's song *Someone Like You* in the Denver airport one day, I realized with tears streaming down my face that the "someone" I had been waiting for my whole life was actually me—my very own soul. As a result, although my spiritual development had long been my priority, my priority now is simply to be me. Not the roles, not the paths—just the soul. When I live from soul, I find I offer all others my best, including my family and those I work with, because I offer them my truth, which is the highest offering I can give.

The first shift toward awakening, then, is to become aware of who we are on the inside and what's truly important to us in the way we express this each and every day. As this awareness dawns within us, we begin to align our external world to match what we are discovering about ourselves.

SHIFT
#2

From Path to No Path

FROM STRAIGHT LINE TO CIRCLE
FROM ADDING TO SHEDDING
FROM KNOWLEDGE TO AWARENESS
FROM COMPLEXITY TO SIMPLICITY

> *There is no path to enlightenment. It lies in all directions at all times. On the journey to enlightenment, you create and destroy your own path with every step.*
> JED MCKENNA

For years I touted a variety of paths up the mountaintop to personal truth, joy, passion, peace, and liberation. While I still feel there can be a time for a path, I surprised myself immeasurably when I discovered that *no path* is where I feel most comfortable and sit today. As I shifted from role to soul, it became clear that inner freedom comes from the open-ended "I Am," with nothing permanently attached to it.

At the same time that my son was beginning to break down his view of himself as primarily an athlete, which occurred during his twelve weeks with a broken wrist, I too was moving—unknowingly at first—from identifying myself as a spiritual seeker as my path to identifying with no path. We mirrored one another and helped each other along, although I didn't fully appreciate this until we arrived at the end of the unraveling process.

For many years on my spiritual journey, I believed that adding more was the point of the game. It seemed to me that more teachings, more books, more workshops, more modalities, more knowledge—in other words, more *becoming*—was how to go about awakening. Some of what I added was beneficial. Then I reached a point where I realized it was time to reverse the process. As I increasingly understood the truth of who I am, which it turned out isn't all that complicated, it all seemed like too much of everything. The different aspects of the journey began to feel heavy, outmoded, and unnecessary. Complexity making way for simplicity now became a vital aspect of my awakening journey.

After nearly twenty-five years as part of the spiritual community, I'm well acquainted with what goes on in that world. On the one hand it's been exciting to see the array of workshops, radio shows, and books that point to the possibility of greater peace, abundance, and fulfillment. On the other hand it started to feel like ruckus to my soul. Many of the spiritual authors I revered began to seem like just another brand. In fact, much of it felt counterintuitive to my awakening journey. Many of the teachings delivered via social media caused my heart to sink, as my mind responded, "Blah, blah, blah." It was as if the teachings were masking the core truth, having become a business. Now they were a barrier to awakening instead of an invitation to awaken further. I realized that sometimes the energy behind a beautiful message shifts. Suddenly, with little fanfare, I just let go of it all—the seeking and the desire to push my career in this field in a direction laid out by others. It wasn't a feeling of being *against* anyone, but more one of being *for* my own soul.

For me these days awakening is less about accumulating and more about letting go—including, ironically, many of the spiritual offerings of the modern world. While I may listen to a speaker every now and then, and discerningly read a handful of books a year, I see clearly that the real work involves streamlining my life to align with my soul rather than to a particular path.

The Ego Likes Defined Paths

Becoming untethered from our ego so that we can better hear and follow the voice of our soul is no small feat. It involves ongoing vigilance, especially in the beginning, to ascertain what stays and what goes. It entails a thorough simplification process that touches every aspect of our lives.

Early on, I became clear that emancipation required evaluating my material possessions, friendships, emotional ties, habits, career, family pursuits, and overall personality-driven pathways. Years into the awakening journey, I was surprised to discover that my spiritual path was one of the things from which I needed emancipating.

While there may be a time for a certain path, fully identifying ourselves with the path is how we become stuck. Like our different roles, paths have a tendency to become crystallized. Lines get drawn in the sand. Unbeknown to us, we begin to inhibit the journey of awakening.

One reason is that paths enable us to feel somewhat settled and secure. We feel like we have somewhere we belong, a place in the scheme of things. The problem with this is that it's the earthy part of us that craves security. Complacency isn't what soul desires, preferring freedom.

Becoming entrenched in one or several paths leads to a narrow perspective on reality and therefore a limited vision of what's possible moment by moment, day by day, and soul to soul. When I made this discovery, I no longer desired to make anything a "thing" in the name of awakening. Instead, I realized that life is what it *is*. I would rather be intensely intimate with what *is* than adhere to a path that may or may not be truly applicable to what I'm experiencing in the now.

Beliefs, isms, practices—these aspects of a path can keep us on the path, but at the expense of keeping us away from soul. For this reason it's worth asking ourselves, "Am I simply adding more knowledge, without truly making headway towards awakening?" Awakening isn't so much a matter of what we know, but is the result of shedding our false layers so that we can live in greater awareness.

Because wholeness stems from less, not more, all aspects of our lives need to be picked through as carefully as a chef at a fine restaurant picks through a mound of shredded crabmeat for shell or through chicken for bones. Don't be afraid to lovingly hack away all that no longer feels as if it's from soul. Often, there is much more than we first realized that can simply be dropped. Once the shedding begins, the marvelous feeling of lightness will be enough to keep the process going until it becomes clear that, on any given day, we are actually living more from soul than role.

Out of the Cocoon

Shifting from path to no path is much like changing from a caterpillar into a butterfly. Once out of the cocoon—awakened, embodied, grown—we know in every cell of our being that we are now truly a butterfly. At this time, we recognize that there is no longer a path to freedom. We *are* free. We are, in fact, freedom itself.

Although my awareness of my soul was for many years tentative, steadily the connection became strong and very much alive, so that now it's always there and never fades even in challenging times. For instance, even when I experienced a nine-month-long total back debilitation that ended in surgery, followed by a melanoma diagnosis only a few short months later, my connection to soul didn't dim. This is true freedom.

To be free means we're able to move in accordance with our internal compass rather than as directed by an external path. We no longer need to follow beliefs that aren't truly ours—and most likely never really were, since most beliefs are embedded within us at an early age with the intention of telling us what's right for us. While we may still be open to the insights of others, our own guidance becomes enough, always. Directed by what stems from our own life experiences rather than the musings of another, we become our own guru and our own role model.

This shift is no longer about the trek up the mountain with its myriad paths ever upward. With this shift, we choose to step off the mountain altogether, take a deep breath, and know simply "I Am," with no tag line. As I've shifted from role to soul, it's become crystal clear to me that inner freedom comes from this open-ended "I Am," with nothing attached to it that lasts more than moment to moment and soul to soul.

Is there anything that could make us "more"? My answer is an emphatic no. There's only growing awareness, so that what's been percolating in us for years at last gushes forth. When we surrender to this, we enjoy a deep knowing that all singular paths lead to the sea in which we're already swimming.

From Role to Soul Leads to No Path

When I was a young child, until about school age, I remember just being Annie without the layers. Over the past several years, flashes of that young girl I once was began coming to me. She was a glorious little creature, open and willing to live from her soul—from no path.

As I, and probably everyone else, grew up, many restrictive qualifiers were added to the feeling of simply "I Am." I learned to tell myself at different times: I am a child, I am a girl, I am a dancer, I am a student, I am a Christian, I am an American, I am a wife, I am a teacher, I am a New Ager, I am a parent, I am a vegan, I am a carnivore, I am an author, I am a spiritual teacher, I am a soul nurturer. You get the idea. As all the labels became more defined, they created more of a solid "thing," which carried with it a rather noisy and heavy feel. The noise and the heaviness built and built until the pressure of the different identities became almost unbearable. Labels, identities, paths—all of these sought to define me.

For this reason, it feels so much better to me right now *not* to identify with any path, any label, any outer form of identity, since such labels often subtly take away my freedom and therefore my power.

Now, instead of being a biker—a pastime I thoroughly enjoy—I choose simply to enjoy pedaling at my own pace and when I feel like it. If I'm inclined to do a fast, athletic ride, I do it. If I feel like having a slow-paced, reflective ride, then that's what I do. Were a race to be brought to my attention, I might or might not train and participate. You see, when it comes to biking, for me there's no path. I feel my way, listen to my body, check the weather, and remain in the now, open and willing but not restricted by a set of rules and beliefs that either I or other bikers have laid down.

As I briefly mentioned in an earlier chapter, from path to no path also applies to my diet. Instead of being either a "vegetarian" or a "carnivore," today I enjoy eating whatever my body feels like eating on any given day. I notice how foods affect me after eating them, and I choose accordingly. In other words, rather than pronouncing anything about my eating habits that I then feel the need to adhere to, I take my cues moment by moment from within. This approach acknowledges the fact that our bodies change, as do our desires, which means it can be counterproductive to adopt a specific dietary path. Even if we've been diagnosed with a disease that requires a distinct way of eating, we can gently shift our habits without turning it into a "thing" to be carried around as a heavy load.

This also works for my politics. Instead of declaring myself a Democrat or a Republican, I remain as open as possible to hearing both sides on specific issues, then listen to my heart when it comes time for action either through my own choices or voting. I have no interest in becoming part of a specific political path, since too often the path becomes more important than the people it purports to be serving. The agendas, the lines drawn in the sand, the strongly held beliefs, and the often ego-driven efforts offered in the vibration of separation hold absolutely no interest for my soul. The path is too loud, the burden too heavy.

As for my "spirituality," again as mentioned earlier, instead of being a lifelong spiritual seeker I'm now content to just be me. I may still prefer certain types of books and speakers over others, and I may still choose to utilize silence and reflection to commune with my soul, but a specific practice or path as "my way" no longer feeds my soul. It feels too constraining and wholly unnecessary. I bless much of what I came to understand on the spiritual path, but also see more clearly now that if held onto too tightly it can be detrimental to awakening.

When we regard our teachers as the "experts," rather than listening intently to the voice of our own soul, any path becomes a barrier to truth. Which is why, asked about her spiritual practice, one well-known author and teacher explained she doesn't have one. She gets up, brushes her teeth, starts her day. Her life is her spiritual practice, and she doesn't even call it spiritual.

Instead of being an author, I now simply enjoy the process of writing. I see that composing a piece is really about the soul expressing itself. Rather than any expectation of how what I write ought to come out, or too much concern as to how it's received by others, I recognize I write because it's a way for me to put my internal world on paper, which in turn helps me to better know myself. If my writing contributes something to others, that's a bonus. I feel no need to be an author who churns out book after book or a blogger who churns out blog after blog. If an idea arises within me, I trust I'll take note and act upon it—not because I'm an author and this is what I'm supposed to do, but because it's being called forth by my soul. In other words, I wait for the inner call instead of allowing the role of "author" to dictate my steps. Even with a full-time career in a particular field going strong, it's important to identify with our soul, not a path. That way, if we're called to be something other than this career requires, we have no difficulty setting down the role.

I've been aware of many shifts throughout my lifetime, and I have always blessed them as the next step. I guess one could say the same thing about this shift to no path. Yet it feels different. As I mentioned earlier, it feels like I stepped off the mountain with its myriad paths upward and am left with simply "I Am."

Feel Your Way

No small number of societies on the planet today are experiencing upheaval from within. The global nature of this upheaval raises the question of whether we are witnessing a breakdown or a breakthrough. From a soul perspective, I feel it's most definitely the latter.

As traditional perceptions of the world and ways of

doing things implode, millions are having to learn to navigate a whole new reality without a sure path. It's definitely no longer business as usual, with the paths as they've always been. Everything is changing, and we must change too if we wish to remain buoyant in our fast-paced, technological, and consciousness-shifting era.

As the paths we used to rely upon are increasingly seen as outdated, and standards and expectations change in the blink of an eye, others' values no longer hold much appeal for me. In a world in which we can create ourselves anew with relative ease, the traditional strict moral codes seem superfluous—all the more so from the perspective of history, with our ability today to gaze back down the corridors of time and note how little peace or enjoyment these old ways brought either the individual or societies as a whole.

The soul perspective offers a *new* way to navigate the folds of life's experiences—though it's not actually new; rather a vantage point that far more of us than ever are now able to adopt. I speak of the utilization of our inner compass, the voice of our own soul. In the changing times in which we live, "feel your way" has become the most used mantra in our home. Feeling our way replaces being on a prescribed path.

How exactly do you feel your way? Let's take the example of decision-making. Take a deep breath, relax into a powerful pause, and listen for the deeper, most purposeful answer *for you*. It will be important to distinguish between old brain patterns, which can be so deeply ingrained as to seem like our authentic voice, and soul. One key to discerning the difference is that, coming from soul, we'll always find ourselves feeling for and moving towards—even if by just a few steps—joy, appreciation, lightness, empowerment, openness, freedom, and love.

If we move in the direction of these feelings in every choice we make—always weighing them against the opposite emotions of heaviness, dread, anxiety, fear, separation, and survival of the fittest—then the correct choice *for us,* meaning a soul-level choice, will become apparent.

Does it take practice to feel our way? Definitely. But the time to start monitoring every choice according to this measurement, instead of making choices prescribed by a path, is now, as we literally throttle at rocket speed into a new and unknown world. To hold onto the old ways of doing things, our former paths, is to risk standing alone grasping for a past that no longer exists.

To get up to speed in feeling your way forward, begin with the smaller decisions you make each day. Go within to discern how you really feel about such simple matters as what to think about, what to talk about, what to read, what to wear, who to spend time with, what music to listen to, what to eat, which movies to see, and how to use your free time.

I'm referring to *every* choice. If you happen to be going through a major life challenge at the moment, it's especially valuable to begin utilizing this approach. Your soul is patiently waiting for you to acknowledge, appreciate, and integrate its gentle guidance. It will show you how to feel your way in each and every situation life presents you with. There's nothing to fear and everything to gain.

Inner resonance, your true compass, is your most valuable asset—hands down and hearts open.

SHIFT

#3

From Outer Symptoms to Inner Signals

FROM LIMITED CONNECTION TO BODY TO INTIMACY WITH
INTELLIGENT SYSTEM
FROM DOCTOR TELL ME TO BODY TELL ME
FROM PHYSICAL LAYER TO ENERGETIC LAYER
FROM LITERAL TO SYMBOLIC

The greatest mistake in the treatment of disease is that there are physicians for the body and physicians for the soul, although the two cannot be separated.
PLATO

In Elizabeth Lesser's *Broken Open*, she talks about a well-known New York City heart surgeon who attended a weekend retreat focused on moving through grief after a loss. At the end of the three-day workshop, he told her that while he physically fixes broken hearts for a living, having mended hundreds over the course of a long career, the true work of mending a malfunctioning heart is the emotional breaking open that can accompany inner work. He then invited her to attend one of his open-heart surgeries, which she did a month later, finding herself moved to her core by the incredible intricacies of the human body. The heart surgeon's point was that our inner being and our physical expression both matter.

Though I'm not a scientist or doctor, health has long been one of my passions. I've learned that both traditional and alternative medicine can be beneficial. But our healthcare systems, while necessary and well-meaning, are only one aspect of the equation. It's also valuable to expand the way we view illness and healing to include a deep personal relationship with our own body in a manner most have never dreamed of. For a person with a blended perspective, whereby the physical is seen as mirroring soul, it's simply not enough to take a drug, undergo surgery, or wear a cast. A blended perspective includes, within any necessary medical intervention, the interior landscape.

For most there's only a limited connection between the physical body and soul. Physical ailments are viewed from a surface perspective, so that a face-value diagnosis directs the treatment and hence the prognosis.

From my vantage point, everything experienced in the human body has a double layer. I now view *all* aspects of health—whether they be what most deem good or bad, joyous or challenging—as having a top physical layer, with all that this entails, including sometimes discomfort and pain, and also an underlying energetic soul layer, which is the larger perspective that holds the key to transformation. To understand this concept is crucial, since the transformation that comes with awakening is our primary reason for being embodied at all.

Most of us have no idea that what has shown up in the body as illness has anything to do with our thoughts, emotions, or beliefs. Even less do we connect illness with the embedded collective consciousness of our era. And even less do we connect illness with fragmented ancestral strands passed down from generation to generation. It's for this reason we approach healing from outside in versus inside out. To truly heal, we can look for a possible root cause that relates to the symptom's location. Symptoms don't just suddenly appear in the body, anymore than a building suddenly appears on the horizon. An inner landscape has a hand in creating both to a certain degree. The body is our dear, dear friend and knows what needs to be explored on the interior.

Through different ailments, I realized years ago that my physical body was going to help me tremendously with my soul lessons. When we are willing to dive deep, symptoms can provide a path to wholeness. They're certainly not the only way, and there's no need to wish for ailments and illnesses in order to grow. But if symptoms develop, the way forward is to acknowledge, befriend, and appreciate them as the soul comrades they are.

Instead of viewing the physical body as separate from what goes on in our (mostly subconscious) inner world, we begin to understand it as an intelligent system made up of smaller intelligent systems, the whole of which works in tandem with soul. This intelligent system (and when I say intelligent, I mean "knowing"), encompassing its individuated systems, mirrors the relationship between oneness and individuated souls. Both are holographic in nature, meaning all smaller aspects also contain the essence of the whole. Our task is to utilize this information to forge an intimate relationship between body and soul. Self-love starts here, and therefore initiating self-healing starts here. Each of us can become deeply aware that our body is a manifestation of our soul. Nobody has the ability to impart this awareness to us.

As Deepak Chopra states in his book *Ageless Body, Timeless Mind*, "The human body, like everything else in the cosmos, is constantly being made anew every second. Although your senses report that you inhabit a solid body in time and space, this is only the most superficial layer of reality. Your body is something far more miraculous—a flowing organism empowered by millions of years of intelligence. This intelligence is dedicated to overseeing the constant change that takes place inside you. Every cell is a miniature terminal connected to the cosmic computer."

Healing from Inside Out

While we often require outside help, it's also true that the physical body's afflictions are a messenger of soul. Once we become aware of the body-soul simpatico, we discover that a treasure trove of information lies directly beneath our physical ailments. This is reason to think twice before simply fighting our symptoms. As a blended being, we can become attuned to the messages our physical home is trying to relay to us about our inner world.

Beyond the medicines, surgeries, and long-term treatment plans, there's almost always emotional excavation to be done. The dis-ease in the body is often a reflection of internal disharmony. Our external symptoms are gateways to internal signals that, when meshed, hold the possibility for healing from the inside out. In other words, when we begin to live from soul rather than simply role, the changes in our body become blessed opportunities for flourishing on all levels. As Rachel Naomi Remen, M.D. shares, "Healing may not be so much about getting better as about letting go of everything that isn't you—all of the expectations, all of the beliefs—and becoming who you are. Not a better you, but a 'realer' you. People can heal and live, and people can heal and die."

Our amazing body has a way of showing us exactly where to look for the causes of illness, which is a means of augmenting a professional view of what has "gone awry" within the body, since an outsider can never be fully privy to our emotions, heart's desires, deeply hidden pain, or subconscious patterns—all of which affect what manifests in our system. Even a genetic predisposition for a particular illness may have an energetic component, sometimes stemming from the ancestral strands of DNA a soul takes on. In this multidimensional reality, there's always more going on than meets the eye.

Let me also hasten to add that there's never a place for blaming ourselves or anyone else for an illness we may be experiencing. Absolutely no blame, and yet, possible energy patterns to consider. And it also must be stated that some illnesses result in physical death even if an energy pattern is recognized and integrated into the whole being. Sometimes the illness simply represents an "exit" strategy for the soul. In other words, the incarnation has served its purpose, it's complete, and on a soul level a new perspective is desired.

Once a symptom appears, it represents the tail end of an energetic trail that may have been building for months, if not years. It's for this reason that inner work is imperative for vibrant health. If a negative emotion (energy in motion) such as anger, guilt, shame, or resentment remains unprocessed, or a true calling or heart's desire remains unexamined and unfulfilled, the suppressed energy will eventually express itself somewhere in the body demanding to be released.

By age five we have usually absorbed many of our subconscious beliefs about who we are and what it will take to be seen, heard, and valued by others. These deeply lodged beliefs often determine much of what later shows up in our relationships, health, and experiences in general. It's for this reason that healing requires us to seek out the gifts hidden in our health challenges, setbacks, and disappointments. Our soul is waiting, with gentle nudges, to expose the hidden aspects of ourselves that we most fear but that offer the greatest possibility for the "peace that passes all understanding" of which a wise person spoke some two millennia ago.

Just how aware are you of the intelligent system that's the sacred vessel you know as your physical body? Do you and your body enjoy the kind of camaraderie you share with a life partner or dear friend? Or do you pay it scant attention, showing it little appreciation, unaware that it thrives when it's not only utilized, but loved and adored by its inhabitant? What a world it would be if each of us walked around comfortable in our body, acknowledging it as a magnificent personal hub of divine expression. Physical, emotional, and mental well-being would abound.

Connectedness to all that occurs with my own body and how it relates to soul is a priority for me day in and day out. I feel totally responsible for my own self-care. I ask for help from outside sources when a concern arises; but right along with external intervention, I maintain accountability for a most intimate relationship with myself. While I encourage you to call on an external healing modality as needed, whether traditional or alternative or both, I suggest you never give over total responsibility for your healing to another. Generally speaking, beyond emergency care, we heal best and most fully from the inside out, and therefore must always remain vigilant in both layers of healing.

A Change of Perspective

For nearly two decades, I felt much more comfortable using alternative medicine and healers rather than traditional doctors. There were two primary reasons for this. One was simply that I have a tremendous passion for the energetic layer. Once I understood around age twenty that there is indeed an energetic imprint for bodily ailments, it thrilled me no end to explore those juicy, unseen aspects of all challenges, including physical ones.

My second reason for leaning in the direction of outside the box healing modalities was a pronounced difference in how I felt when leaving the two types of appointments. After leaving my primary care doctor or a traditional specialist, I often felt somewhat unseen and unheard, even diminished, if not confused. I was disappointed by the unwillingness, if not inability, of many a professional to swim with me in the deeper waters of my interior world. On the other hand, when leaving a more holistic practitioner, I almost always felt uplifted, fully heard and seen, and whole. I also had a clearer understanding of *my* part in what was occurring in my own body. These appointments are where I learned how to connect the dots between outer symptoms and inner signals, eventually leading me to do much of the detective work on my own. In other words, soul was taken into consideration, becoming very much a part of the solution.

The human fear of death and the soul's enthusiasm for evolution share the same space. The upshot of this is that an almost joyous feeling of adventure can coexist with discomfort, fear, and pain. By creating a deep and loving friendship between soul and body, we develop a two-way communication that allows our internal and external worlds to work together in a masterful partnership that results in greater truth.

We likely all have a measure of psychic debris that's no longer needed and is just waiting to be set free, and we have a physical body willing to deliver the means. The body offers a red light-green light navigational system unique to each individual. Know your own signals and what they mean in relationship to what's occurring in your life. The body is privy to all that occurs, and feels the truth with more accuracy than the mind. Listen to the cues from your body.

In my years of self-exploration, it was only when I developed an open, loving, and intimate relationship with both my body and its soul source that I was able to ignite the self-love I had always sought. It turns out that greater intimacy with our body is the gateway to increased intimacy with our soul. Both sit quietly waiting for us to consciously make the connection. If we don't, illness may well give us a nudge.

Body Awareness: A Few Points to Consider

It's important to acknowledge emotions as they arise on the front end of an experience by accepting and allowing them to be fully felt without telling ourselves we should feel something other than what we feel. The "spiritual" experience of transcending the body advocated by many isn't necessary, since the body offers the greatest opportunity to become more intimate with our soul. Feelings are felt within the body. Instead of seeking to transcend the body, we need to create a lifelong friendship with it through dialogue, touch, and quiet appreciation for all it offers so readily and lovingly.

If a specific body part is under duress, we can initiate self-healing through loving, daily communication with this body part. It helps to get up close and personal with it several times a day so that the body understands there's love and support flowing its way from an appreciative friend, rather than ire and resentment from an unaware stranger. Express heartfelt understanding that the cells of this specific body part are working hard to heal for the good of the whole. Ensure them that their efforts aren't unnoticed.

Sexuality and sensuality are to be honored, celebrated, and openly expressed rather than shamefully hidden. While the sexual act is private, the fact we are sexual beings who appreciate and enjoy sex serves us best when we don't suppress it, whether straight or gay. Masturbation is a natural aspect of sexuality, and from a young age children can appreciate its normalcy and feel comfortable touching *any* part of their own body with love and tenderness. One of the most important discussions we can have with our children, beginning with digestible bites at an early age, is an invitation to view their own body as a treasured gift that's theirs to befriend, nurture, and enjoy.

It's valuable to express our soul freely through our body by dancing, hugging, touching, kissing, singing, walking, laughing—any means of self-expression that enhances the quality of our life. Let a deep respect for the relationship between body and soul create a conscious aspect to each breath and action. In addition to action, utilize dreams, journaling, and quiet reflection to support all aspects of the body-soul relationship. This helps us to love our body dearly for the gift that it is, regardless of whether its size or shape conforms to standards society regards as "normal."

Loving your body right now, just as it is, coupled with enthusiasm for creating healthy changes if desired, is an important aspect of forging a deeply fulfilling experience of life.

Symptoms as Signals

My greatest passion in both my work and personal life is helping people who are open and ready to see themselves in a multidimensional light. This is certainly not new work, as thousands upon thousands of teachers have offered the same message for millennia. Yet for the first time in human history, it feels totally available to *all* from everyday sources, such as myself, in language that can be readily shared.

Like bees to nectar, individuals from all over the planet are shifting from a primarily left-brain, rational, analytical focus to a balance that includes an intuitive, whole, soul-centered (right-brain) approach to life and death. Perhaps one of the dimensions of life in which this shift is occurring most rapidly is that of health. While the left brain tends to perceive illness and healing as a physical and chemical issue, we are being urged by right brain energy to take a closer look at what ails us. More and more research points to the multifaceted nature of health, and in my work I'm seeing a desire on the part of many to address the root layer of illness rather than merely "treating" it symptomatically.

This approach applies to all of life's challenges. The script, venue, supporting players, unique plots, and scenes—such as a failed relationship, a confrontation with a friend, a health malady—are simply manifestations that offer clues to lead us to take a closer look at our core issues. No two cases are alike, no two inner signals identical, even though the outer symptoms may appear similar.

In my own case, for over a year and a half after having my second child exactly sixteen months after my first, I developed horrific eczema on my lower legs—the bloody welts kind that left me cranky, embarrassed, and exhausted. After five different dermatologists and numerous tubes of steroid creams that offered only temporary relief, I knew I had to take a closer look at what was really ailing me. Through synchronicity, I was led to a hypnotherapist. At the age of twelve, I had experienced the healing of warts through this same therapy. Following a three-hour appointment focused on what lay beneath my eczema, I experienced an epiphany while soaking in a hot bath. I wept as I understood the emotional root of the affliction.

I had given up my teaching career to stay home with my children. While it was a choice I deeply desired, I felt I was no longer standing on my own two feet financially. In other words, there was disharmony in my choice that needed to be acknowledged and released. In this case it only took a few days for the eczema to disappear and never return. The answer didn't lie in going back to work, but in resolving the emotional disharmony that not working had triggered.

On another occasion I contracted laryngitis the day before my stepbrother's wedding extravaganza weekend. It resolved the day I returned home from my trip. At the time, we were still meshing families—a new marriage for my dad that involved adult children, along with other dynamics that were new to me. A part of me felt I couldn't express my truth, so I kept my feelings inside and went along with what was expected of me. I knew when I lost my voice at this important family event—our first since my dad remarried—that the laryngitis represented my failure to speak up in a more forthright manner. All these years later, I remember those four days vividly. It was so painful to speak that I spent most of the weekend simply nodding my head.

Several years ago, after working closely with a man my age who was dying of pancreatic cancer, I knew intuitively that something was off in my visceral section. No traditional doctor could detect through tests that anything was amiss, but three different medical intuitives saw the same thing, which matched what I was feeling. It was the beginning of an unhealthy energy pattern in my abdomen. One of these healers placed me on a strict vegan diet for three months to create more alkalinity and less acidity in my body. During this time an underlying theme of my life surfaced: extreme empathy. Several months later, with a deepened relationship with my visceral section—which was now filled with acknowledgment, appreciation, and actual knowledge of that particular area of my body—while driving on a cold but vibrant January day, I knew I was healed.

I went back to my medical intuitives for confirmation, and indeed the darker energy enfolding my liver and pancreas had dissipated—an energy that in a dream I understood would have given me some "big" trouble a decade or so later. In this case, the energetic pattern was discovered on the front end rather than the back end, the direction we all hope to head with our healing.

During my recent nine-month lower back issue that ended with surgery, as a nerve was wrapped around a bulging disc, my relationship with and love for my body intensified greatly. Never before had I been forced to be so gentle with my own body as I simultaneously sought out what the nerves and tissue in my lower back and left leg were trying to tell me. It was a prolonged period of pain like I had never known. While I could have had the surgery sooner, there was an unstoppable desire within me to grow from the experience, juicing it for soul development—an approach that seemed odd to many. I knew that expansion was at hand, so I was willing to forego the ease of movement and to live in pain to uncover what these symptoms wanted me to understand about myself.

Beyond the x-rays, MRI, Watsu water therapy, osteopathic manipulation, and increased glucosamine and calcium intake, among other protocols, I listened to my sacral region and the nerve that ran like fire down my left leg. I listened to my own soul and what I sought to understand more deeply about myself. Through the tears and fears, I came to know myself better in so many ways.

This particular health challenge led me down a multi-layered and well-hidden interior path that ultimately offered me freedom from a lifelong pattern embedded in me from childhood—hence the sacral area—first chakra that represents my past. This was a pattern of playing small, flying under the radar, never factoring myself in ahead of others, and basically many tentacles of that good old extreme empathy perspective mentioned earlier that had been passed down on my maternal side for generations. In line with my own experience, a general feeling in the self-exploratory community is that women are often called to do soul work in search of self-love and the capacity to factor themselves in, as well as to learn to receive love more freely. Men, on the other hand, often answer the call to learn to open their hearts, empathize, and give love more freely. While not a steadfast rule, it seems there's truth to the generalization.

Just as I was beginning to soar with my new work as a soul nurturer and writer, my past simply reared up and said, "Not so fast, sister." It actually felt like I was being pulled flat on my back by a huge cord during this period. The psychic debris from my distant past was endeavoring to have its say, and I was finally ready to be still and listen, becoming attuned to the deeply ingrained messages of childhood about what it means to be a "good" girl.

From my own experience and that of friends, I've learned that if you lose your voice, examine what you might be unwilling or afraid to express. If your knee blows out in an injury, ask yourself what you are no longer willing to hold up and support. If your wrist breaks, consider where you might become more flexible in life. If your eye begins to twitch, look within to see how you might perceive things in a new light. If your head aches, ponder the ways in which you might not be fully feeling your emotions. If you have dental issues, think about the ways in which having to maintain a "stiff upper lip" may not behoove you.

The body doesn't want to be in pain or symptomatic, but it's an all-knowing system willing to be the trigger for soul development.

Three Biopsies and Two Layers of Perspective

In the days when I was deciding whether to have neurosurgery on my back, I was weighing my options while driving one day, when I suddenly received a message via the familiar surge of oneness that brings tears to my eyes, making me aware that *everything* is in the oneness—both the neurosurgeon and the unconventional healer.

Following back surgery, I adopted a more balanced approach to medicine. While my great love over the past twenty years has been the underlying deeper layer of what a symptom symbolizes, I felt I ought to pay greater attention to the physical layer, given I was now over forty. This led me to make a slew of allopathic appointments that included the dermatologist, eye doctor, gynecologist, and radiologist for a mammogram.

My willingness to trot to these traditional medical practices with an upbeat click in my step surprised even myself. In the dermatologist's office, I remembered at the last minute to ask her to look at a mole on my upper back thigh, an area that rarely sees the sun. I thought nothing of it due to its location and my olive complexion. She didn't like the look of it, and it was promptly removed and biopsied.

A few days later on the morning of my afternoon mammogram, the dermatologist called to say that unfortunately the mole tested as a stage one malignant melanoma, and that I needed to remove further tissue. Then my mammogram and ultrasound turned up a mass in my right breast—thankfully, I learned almost a week later, a benign fibroadenoma. The surgical procedure to remove tissue from my leg required thirteen stitches, followed by a visit to the dermatologist every three months for the next two years.

For those of you focused on the top layer of physicality, I encourage you to also explore the layer that lies just beneath physical ailments, since it's ripe with possibilities for coming to know soul more deeply. For those who have moved fully into the realm of energy medicine, make sure it isn't to the exclusion of the physical. Awakening to ourselves as embodied souls requires attentiveness to our whole being.

The bottom line is that if we choose to take on a physical body, there will be physical challenges, and likely lots of them. We can open, soften, and become more aware from them; or we can close, harden, and shrink.

Baseball, A Broken Wrist, and Ten Things to Consider

Physical injuries and illnesses can be especially challenging when they concern our children. They can also be enlightening, both for our children and ourselves.

As they say, timing is everything—and as they say in certain sports, it's all in the wrist. I mentioned earlier that my twelve-year-old son broke his wrist at a basketball tournament, four weeks almost to the minute from the fulfillment of his dream to play baseball with his travel team for a six-day extravaganza at Cooperstown, the youth baseball mecca where the Baseball Hall of Fame is located. If you have a young boy who plays baseball, chances are he shares the same dream.

To say that my son was upset would be putting it mildly. To say that we, as his parents, weren't heartbroken for him would be a lie. Even his eighty-two-year-old grandfather, his namesake and a professional baseball player for seventeen years, was teary eyed when told the news.

Where awareness is concerned, some important understandings bobbed to the surface, slowly making this unexpected and seemingly negative turn of events not only acceptable but rife with possibility. Having said this, I need to stress that while there are always much more devastating situations than what we may be experiencing, it's important not to let this realization diminish or invalidate the feelings at hand. The disappointment, sadness, and pain must be felt without feeling ashamed because others have it worse. Our experience is sacred and to be valued as tailor-made for our own development.

I mentioned the timing of this injury. Valuable insights can be dredged from a situation by paying attention to the timing. Also, what we will miss as a result of the change in our circumstances is a clue to our underlying fears and beliefs. *Identification* and *attachment* are two of the key areas to dissect. The more acute the loss is, the greater the opportunity to experience a different perspective. Beneath all the cloaks of ego, we are infinite beings. Letting go of holding on too tightly to a one-dimensional way of identifying ourselves creates a wider, deeper vantage point—and a more accurate one.

There's no question but that my son was born an athlete. Even as a young boy he exhibited fluidity in his physical movements. He identifies with his athleticism more than with any other aspect of himself. Others identify him in this way also. To navigate life from a different perspective, especially during a season when he stood out as a talented athlete, was a profound shift for him. I had to acknowledge that it represented a shift for me also, since I felt attachment to my son as a gifted athlete, identifying *myself* through him in some ways and feeling disappointment not only for him but also for me.

The location of the injury—the wrist—represented flexibility, which was an issue for our son. Acceptance of the ups and downs of our humanness was an important aspect of this occurrence.

We talked earlier about conscious participation in our own healing. I was astounded not only by the lack of warmth but also the lack of insight into a holistic approach on the part of a renowned orthopedic hand specialist. Not one mention of nutritional aid for mending a bone. I'm referring to such obvious steps as increasing magnesium, zinc, and calcium phosphate intake; increasing fruit, vegetable, and protein intake; no soda, which depletes; no ibuprofen, which inhibits bone growth after swelling goes down; and not just milk alone, but vitamin C to help with absorption. None of this figured into the allopathic approach. Not to mention visualization of the bone mending, which is another terrific way of taking ownership of our healing. And of course, not a hint of becoming more intimate with the wrist in an openly expressed, if only privately in the mind, dialogue of love and gratitude for all that a healthy wrist allows. Much can be done energetically that few of us fully understand, such as inviting the wrist to heal.

Much can also be gained from observing rather than always actively participating. By simply watching, my son picked up a lot at practices and games with regard to how he relates to others, how peers interact, how coaches teach, and the nuances of the sport. He eventually voiced many observations, letting us know that his well of compassion and empathy had expanded. His appreciation of himself, his body, others, and the game of baseball grew by leaps and bounds because his wrist snapped. Once we were assured the wrist was going to heal, it became apparent that the break was secondary to the development that was possible.

A Bite on the Ass

When I was fairly new to blogging, I wrote a blog that elicited a favorable response from many and an angry onslaught from a few. Although my position was one of neutrality, I quickly realized that even neutrality is a personal perspective—one that many don't enjoy. Eventually I removed the post, joking to my husband, "That blog really came back to bite me on the ass!"

It so happened we were going to Florida on vacation. Three days into my trip, I awoke with a bite of some kind—a spider, a scorpion, who knows? The bite created a welt four inches by two on my right butt cheek. It became a daily ritual each morning for all ten family members aboard the Burnside holiday train to check on The Bite.

The Big Bite on My Ass lasted for the entire trip and

remained for several days after as a slightly pink expanse that, thankfully, eventually stopped itching. Initially it had purple streaks in it, and the lymph node in my right groin swelled as my body fought to release the toxins and the negativity.

Since I always look for deeper meaning in my physical ailments, I laughed out loud in the shower as I made the correlation. My belief that my blog had come back to bite me on the ass manifested in a physical bite on the ass! The soul perspective always reminds us to be conscious of thoughts, words, deeds, and beliefs. In more secular terms, be careful what you wish for because you just might get it.

My bite on the butt reminded me that the whole of life is an interwoven fabric, an underlying oneness expressed in a world of diversity. Since everything is a manifestation of this oneness, everything that happens to us is a means of coaxing us into awareness of the oneness. So what can there ever really be that needs healing? From the vantage point of oneness, no healing is actually necessary, since even sickness is the oneness at work to awaken us to our blended state. In absolute terms, there can never be any separation from the oneness. Our task, then, is to see ourselves as an individuated expression of the oneness in this space-time continuum, which increasingly brings our essential wholeness into every area of our everyday lives.

SHIFT

#4

From Woe Is Me to Grow Is Me

FROM DARK NIGHT TO INCREASED LIGHT
FROM EXTERIOR TO INTERIOR
FROM DENIAL TO TRUSTING THE TRIGGER
FROM SHADOW TO ILLUMINATION
FROM EMBEDDING EMOTIONS TO FEELING EMOTIONS FULLY

*So long as the finger is pointed outward,
I stay trapped in my web.*
JAYSON GADDIS

One of my favorite sayings is *Grow is Me rather than Woe is Me*. From the perspective of soul, no experience is too small or too mundane to ignite expanded awareness, since everything is after all in the oneness. From a blended perspective, life's circumstances, experiences, and relationships provide the fodder for awakening if we are willing to look at the underlying layers of each of these aspects of our lives.

When we become more awakened, all kinds of change can be seen as an opportunity to know ourselves more fully. The external world with its myriad of ups and downs becomes an ongoing opportunity to deepen our relationship with our own soul. Inner work proves gratifying even while we are going through something disappointing, upsetting, or tragic. Sometimes a dark night of the soul, or several smaller difficult experiences, brings us to our knees and causes us to journey within. However, it doesn't have to be this way—and more and more the collective consciousness is creating the space to awaken in a less suffering-filled manner.

Initially inner work, also known as shadow work, may consist of learning about the shadows, wounds, and false beliefs that lurk in our subconscious. For many this becomes a path for a while as they seek to clear psychic debris from their inner landscape by making it conscious and integrating it into their lives. This is important work, but not work we need to be stuck in forever. Eventually, our own life lived from soul rather than role, moment to moment and day by day, becomes sufficient to navigate all of our experiences. When this happens, *Grow is Me rather than Woe is Me* becomes our preferred state.

Until we crack ourselves open enough to consciously delve into our unconscious aspects, we remain tethered to them. In many ways they run our life, though we may not realize it. The good news is that when we're ready to look at our shadow, the external world provides every trigger and clue we need to how our wholeness can emerge. In this light, human hardship is seen as a positive that can expedite soul excavation. A *Grow is Me* perspective requires us to be accountable for our choices, so that our external landscape flows from our soul.

After years of shadow work—which is an aspect of the spiritual path I resisted for a long time—I now find myself enjoying a natural rhythm between my inner and outer realities, whereby I readily connect outer circumstance to my internal landscape. Being attuned to the exchange between the inner and the outer doesn't mean we don't experience painful emotions; rather, it means we feel what needs to be felt on the spot or soon after, then allow it to pass right on through. Generally speaking, an external happenstance that draws out an emotional reaction is a signal our interior contains a spot that's ready to be illuminated, owned, and integrated into our wholeness. If we pay attention to how we feel, we'll know when and where to look, since our own life always leads the way.

Liberation from the underlying ties that bind us means trusting the triggers as they come to our awareness, rather than feeling the prick or the deep gash and stuffing it down to linger and eventually wreak emotional and perhaps physical havoc. This is what I like to call front end work rather than back end work. I've learned that it's empowering to acknowledge and work through a trigger, since it enables me to recover trapped energy.

Before sharing some personal examples of what I'm talking about, I want to point out the difference between emotional triggers, which are a signal that a shadow aspect has been touched upon, and feelings, which highlight a soul-based connection to the oneness. Both can be felt within the body. Emotional triggers are typically based on old pain, past conditioning, false beliefs, and judgment of an experience as either good or bad. Some situation arises that sets off a wave of emotion we perceive as negative. If we are aware of what's happening, we don't suppress such emotion. Neither do we necessarily vent it. Rather, we acknowledge it, allowing it to be, whereupon in due course it passes. This can happen in seconds, minutes, hours, days, or even months, depending on the nature of the emotion. For example, grief over the death of a loved one will require much longer to pass than anger over an offensive remark.

Feelings are often confused with emotions as if they were the same. However, I find that feelings are of a different quality, being soul expressions of the oneness moving through the body. They are experienced as a deep connection to the oneness and lead to a greater awareness of our true nature as an individuated aspect of this oneness. Feelings offer us a taste of a blended love-awe-gratitude state of being. The more we become aware of our emotional triggers, so that we simply observe the emotion as it arises and then dissipates, the more we open ourselves to the deeper feelings that arise beyond typical human emotion.

What I Do When I'm Triggered

In terms of my emotional triggers, my experience has been one of moving in and out of the woods. I find that each time I'm triggered, if I remain aware, the time in the woods becomes less scary, less all-encompassing, and less enduring. "This too shall pass" becomes more and more apparent as a universal truth.

To illustrate, my parents separated when I was nineteen years old, eventually divorcing. This was my first major dark night of the soul, my first conscious cracking open—although, looking back from what I know now, there were many more subtle experiences throughout childhood that invited inner reflection. The effects of the divorce lasted several years and involved emotions such as confusion, self-doubt, and grief. It was so overwhelming that it catapulted me onto a path of self-exploration, which led eventually to a place deep within where self-love is experienced as an expression of ultimate oneness.

On another occasion, an experience of working with an individual who died triggered seemingly everything I had ever feared about myself—shame, vulnerability, unworthiness, and weakness. During the two years that followed, I surrendered more of my layers—mask and beliefs—than I knew existed. This particular experience brought me face to face with death, and in due course to the realization that death isn't the end.

Along the way there have been countless disagreements with friends, some small and a handful big and long-lasting, each triggering in me an aspect of my shadow that has to do with not speaking my truth forthrightly, thinking I was protecting the feelings of others. It was instilled in me at a young age that to be a good girl, I must people-please, be non-confrontational, offer pleasantries, skirt around issues, and respond diplomatically to everything that came my way, even if I was being bullied. A need to explain and justify myself kept me mired in endless repetitious patterns with others. Years of work on this particular aspect of my shadow led me to factor myself in and create boundaries. I now choose my energy exchanges much more carefully, speaking from my heart. I learned that just because an interaction has been initiated by another doesn't mean we must conform to it. We can choose to pass, opting instead for calmness, peace, ease, and flow.

Another aspect of my shadow was exposed while I was writing my first book, when my initial experience with an editor triggered an awareness of my tendency to surrender my power to others, especially those I perceive as experts. Even toward the close of my first interaction with this editor, I experienced a negative reaction in my body. Her more masculine, abrasive approach felt like a stark contrast to my naturally feminine, nurturing way of being. Despite the warning signals, I chose to utilize her skills, since other authors in my field had used her—only to learn what it feels like to become disempowered. Not only did I begin to question everything I'd written, as well as the very premise of my book, but the process cost me a lot financially—more than agreed upon. Just like my power, the excess was extracted without my consent via a credit card. I felt burned, and it took me weeks before I mustered the courage to reach out to another editor who was a better fit. Through this experience some mighty fine soul work was accomplished. I've given away my power in smaller ways since, but never again to that degree. I'm more able to deal with a situation on the front end rather than the more painful and laborious back end.

Because I naturally enjoy "being" over "doing," for a long time I nevertheless felt a need to generate busyness in order to consider myself productive. One day, while exasperated with my daughter, I accused her of being lazy. No sooner were the words out of my mouth than I realized I had triggered a deep-seated fear that I'm actually really, really lazy. I had no idea I disliked and feared this possibility so intensely. But after befriending this aspect of my shadow, I recognized that my ability to step out of constant activity, sit on a park bench, relax, and enjoy lots of downtime is one of my most treasured and useful characteristics. As mentioned earlier, I'm task-specific and accomplish what needs to be taken care of as it arises. Owning "lazy" that day made a huge difference in the way I perceive myself, adding a dollop of grace to my growing self-love.

When I'm triggered, as soon as possible I carve out time for quiet and stillness. As I become aware of the external cue, I point it back at myself, examining my interior to see if it reveals some unintegrated issue. I weigh both the light and the dark aspects of whatever may be exposed.

If I find myself becoming annoyed, even angered, by an overly aggressive individual, I look at my anger to see what I might be angry about in *myself*. Could it be that I, too, can be aggressive in my approach? Or is the anger towards myself because I'm seeing more clearly that I'm not sufficiently assertive? If I find it's the former, the positive side of this is that at least I'm willing to speak up for myself, even if in a more intense tone than I enjoy being spoken to. When I'm not assertive, the light side is that

I'm a good listener who doesn't always feel the need to interject an opinion.

To integrate an aspect of our shadow, it can be helpful to become aware of the condition in our childhood that established this dimension of our shadow, as most life themes can be traced back to childhood. This doesn't mean thinking of ourselves as still a child, for we aren't. To do so only keeps us stuck, pandering to our immature wish to behave like a child and be treated like a child. It means seeing the difference between the way we reacted as children and the way we need to respond as mature adults. The contrast can be painful, but facing up to it is precisely the self-confrontation required to mature.

Our shadow shouldn't be feared. Discovering aspects of the shadow can be both exhilarating and liberating. Having said this, we don't want to be in "shadow work mode" all the time, digging for new aspects of our shadow and turning the whole enterprise into another "thing." Instead, we utilize our own life consciously lived to uncover aspects of the shadow as they arise in reaction to an emotional trigger. It becomes not a big to-do, but part of the natural rhythm of life.

As work with an emotional trigger comes to a close, we typically feel lighter, experience less judgment, and enjoy greater self-love. We know ourselves a little bit wider and deeper, and our soul smiles.

My High School Reunion and the Unexpected Week that Followed

When I attended my 25th High School Reunion, it had been fifteen years since I had been back to my hometown for a reunion without bringing either my spouse or children. A huge impetus for attending this particular reunion was to spend time with two of my closest friends, one of whom had remained in the area and the other of whom lived on the opposite coast. These gals are what I call lifelong, deathbed friends. Our connection remains inviolate—a well of shared experiences, familiarity, and love. Time spent in coffee klatches, talking, eating, dancing, and walking was the highlight of the weekend.

I want to preface what I have to share about this reunion concerning my shadow by saying that many go home and don't feel anything deeper than the outer layers of their interactions, whereas others feel the edges of the shadow but shove them back down into the darkness. Then there are those who choose to return only rarely to their roots due to either a conscious or subconscious understanding that psychic debris from childhood looms large in such a setting, and they simply never want to "go there." What I share here isn't in any way about other people, but about my experience and what it showed me about myself. On some level I've long understood the saying, "You can never go home again." Now I felt the truth of this deep in my bones.

As excited as I was about my trip, as the time drew near, I also felt an uneasiness. I remember thinking that something in need of clearing was going to surface. Peering into unacknowledged corners of our psyche that nevertheless have a tremendous effect on our beliefs, choices, and actions is never the "go to" activity for a good time. During the course of the weekend an energy pattern from my childhood got dredged up and reflected back to me several times. But I was no longer a child picking up this energy and inculcating it unprocessed to be regurgitated in dysfunctional behavior. Feeling the energy pattern as a conscious adult devoted to self-awareness and care of my soul was painful.

When I sat on the plane home, with the setting sun shimmering on the water surrounding an area that has always been close to my heart, I felt I might burst into tears. The sense of grief was overwhelming. I knew I was in for a long week as I examined both the dark and light aspects of the experience.

As the week progressed, I spent time in solitude, acknowledging the energy pattern as part of who I am today. With both tears and appreciation, I recalled different stages of my development, allowing myself to get "up close and personal" with an aspect of my past I hadn't fully owned. This processing and integration became my priority until the energy tied up in it had been released. With it, another chunk of shadow receded.

Becoming a Clear Mirror for My Children

As we are all mirrors for one another, reflecting back aspects of each other's internal landscapes, imagine the huge interchange that's occurring energetically in the parent-child relationship. Just beneath the surface of our lovely masks lurk some not-so-lovely beliefs, patterns, and perspectives—imprints that no longer serve our highest good, much less the highest good of our beloved children or the world at large. Unintentionally, and often unknowingly, we offer these dense traits to our children simply by being in their presence, quite apart from the things we say and do.

While many of us tend to look outside ourselves for "expert" answers when things go awry with our children—always in search of the perfect parenting strategy so that we can become the best head honcho we can be—it has become apparent to me that the greatest gift we can offer our children is to be a clear mirror. The mirror many of us offer our children is a blurry, gray, cracked mirror that can't possibly reflect back to them the whole, creative, and powerful beings they are as their birthright. Consequently working from both the inside out and from the outside in towards a full expression of our own magnificent wholeness benefits our children more than any pedagogical method or behavior modification system ever could.

To really "homerun" a clear mirror, I enlist the help of Lao-Tzu, with whom in my dreams I've conversed atop a mountain on many a day. His beautiful message has been posted in our home for over sixteen years: "If there is right in the soul, there will be beauty in the person. If there is beauty in the person, there will be harmony in the home. If there is harmony in the home, there will be order in the nation. If there is order in the nation, there will be peace in the world."

Part of becoming a clear mirror is to forgive ourselves. Forgiveness is simply another word for freedom, empowerment, and peace for the soul. None of us are perfectly clear mirrors, and it's important to be forgiving of ourselves for this.

You'll notice that I said forgiving of *ourselves*. I learned that forgiveness matters primarily for us, as the negative energy embedded in our system due to anger, guilt, and resentment ultimately affects mostly us, and only to some extent the ones who must interact with us if they allow it. Forgiveness, always extended towards ourselves first, allows the free-flow of vitality to resume its natural course through our heart, mind, and body, enabling us to untether ourselves from unnecessary suffering so that we have the energy to create our desired reality. Release, in the form of forgiving, is a choice and can become a daily practice.

Forgive both people *and* situations. The objective is always to work through emotions *as they occur* rather than holding, denying, or stuffing down negative energy to be looked at later through dis-ease in the body or some other disheartening situation that mirrors the original situation—same basic script, different players. What we resist does indeed persist, hampering the full expression of soul.

The shift into a growth mode by facing up to our

shadow whenever life reflects it back to us inaugurates a lifelong journey with no finish line, highlighted by frequent moments of illumination and deeply felt authenticity as we move step by step beyond the limitations of our roles.

SHIFT
#5

From Busyness Without to Stillness Within

FROM COMPULSIVE MIND CHATTER TO DEEP LISTENING
FROM PERPETUAL ACTION TO THOUGHTFUL ACTION
FROM NEAR CONSTANT DOING TO MORE FREQUENT BEING
FROM NON-STOP TALKING TO INTENTIONAL HEARING

*Keep what is worth keeping and with the breath
of kindness blow the rest away.*
DINA CRAIK

Mary Oliver famously wondered, "Tell me, what is it you plan to do with your one wild and precious life?"

Our culture makes busyness, productivity, and accomplishment badges of honor. The question to ask ourselves is, "What exactly are we busy doing?" Or is it another "should" based on societal norms or past conditioning? Are we wasting precious hours trapped in a largely unfulfilling life of our own design?

At one time a weekly manicure may have served a need and been a good fit for us, and yet it may not be as empowering for us today. Something as seemingly harmless as a weekly lunch date with a friend, several trips to the gym each week, or even a meditation class may need to be evaluated for whether it adds a layer to our busyness that impedes living from soul rather than role.

In other words, awakening requires becoming clear about what serves us on a deeper level, which involves identifying what holds us back. Just as we clean out our closets, we must reshape our waking hours so that we're living true, in that our interior matches our exterior. Taking a close look—and I do mean *close*—at our everyday activities is imperative. Only we can determine the different layers of busyness that shroud our core.

Obviously, living as a blended being, and especially for those of us raising a family, we must earn some type of a living. Certain chores must be tended to on a regular basis for life to run smoothly. But beyond our basic needs, which can usually be streamlined more than we realize, busyness isn't something that happens *to* us. Rather, it's an ongoing "chaos" we consciously and unconsciously create for a multitude of reasons, the main one being *our fear of intimacy with our own soul.*

The call of this chapter is to own our busyness by choosing what's most meaningful to soul, then without guilt, shedding the superfluous. The honing process involves recognizing what feeds our ego and what feeds our soul, then joyfully choosing soul more and more, which results in a balanced life that honors the totality of our humanity.

Is it going be one more errand to purchase more stuff? Or a walk immersed in the beautiful fall colors, opening up the space for a creative idea to take root or a longed-for marital insight to dawn? Is it going to be another workshop espousing how to find a soul mate? Or spending more time communing with our own soul? There's no right or wrong answer to these rhetorical questions. They are simply a way of discovering which of our day-to-day choices may be holding us back. We too often forget that busyness, even in the modern world, is a choice—an all-important "way of life" choice—and that we are captains of our own rat race.

To make the shift to a soul-driven life, we must first acknowledge time spent in our rich inner world as not only valuable but a necessity, akin to breathing. The pure joy of soul contemplation without an objective is powerful. The point is to reflect without feeling it has to involve shadow work or interior excavation, but just seeing what arises.

Reflection and contemplation are undervalued in western culture, yet they are of paramount importance to the state of the world at large—so much so that we all need to make them a priority. In this way our external world comes to reflect the peace and joy of our soul center.

Being and Doing

My husband and I have always emphasized to our children that no matter what career path they choose, how they are "being" while they are working is as important as what they are doing. If they choose to work as a hairdresser, engineer, cook, or teacher, the *texture* of what they offer will have a greater impact than the work itself. The primary issue is whether they are aware and authentic in their efforts and interactions.

In today's fast-moving world, it's no longer acceptable to comfortably sit back and unconsciously create from a place of ignorance of our responsibility and accountability for what occurs in our own reality. Every individual matters as we seek to evolve the entire planet to a higher consciousness. To do so, we each need to recognize the source of our own power to create freely from inside out, without the imagined external constraints of bygone eras. The world has changed, and we must change with it by moving into a deeper understanding and expression of our individual power to shape what we see in the external world.

Many just go, go, go. Such individuals produce mainly from their physical and mental drive without tapping into soul, thereby missing the opportunity to be of great benefit to others through what they produce. Communing with soul allows us to assemble the pieces in the most advantageous way for everyone involved. This aspect of the creative process is extremely important, as we are allowing ourselves to work on a deeper plane. As we begin to create from both the heart and an inner knowing of who we *really* are as integral, powerful aspects of a divine whole so magnificent that we cannot fully wrap our minds around it, we become higher versions of ourselves, growing into our potential and thereby fulfilling our soul's intended mission.

If we can infuse our habits and work efforts—both necessary aspects of creating a desired reality—with a more fluid, relaxed, open, and joyous flow, we move *into* our interior power and expand exponentially our capacity to create beyond often limited expectations. Most of us don't perceive ourselves to be anywhere near the powerful creators we truly are. More often than not, we condemn ourselves to pushed, contrived, narrow results that are so much less than what we are capable of offering to ourselves and the world at large.

A major life theme of mine has been balancing being, reflection, meditation, and non-doing with doing in the form of networking, producing, and so on. Since the tendency is to lead a life based on one or the other, we need to consciously find a way to blend and balance the two in a rhythm that works best for us.

In my work and life in general, I've learned to bless both the pauses and the starts. My creative surges and heady motion are wonderful. I value the inspired movements and the synchronicities. Yet it's the quiet moments that really provide the inspiration and allow for the carvings in the canyon. When there's a pause, don't for a moment question whether you're doing something wrong. On the contrary, build in pauses, both throughout the day and over the course of a week, a month, and a year.

I can now more readily identify a call to action, as well as the inevitable call to non-action—a skill I gained the hard way. For instance, on one occasion, I was raring to go, with ideas and energy surging. Since I'd planned to meditate, I ignored the energy and sat in silence. It didn't go well. I was in a creative vortex that was ready to be expressed. In fact, it felt like my energy wanted to jump right through my skin. It definitely wasn't a time for non-action. When manifestation is at the ready, we shouldn't pause a single moment. If you are feeling creative, let it flow. At other times when there's no flow, instead of forcing it, enter into stillness, which will in due course relax you into a powerful action phase.

The waterfront and sunlight help me to become clear. I'm exceptionally open to guidance from my sacred wholeness in such an environment. For this reason, except when in college, I've always lived near a large body of water. My inactive times frequently involve time spent where I can commune with my soul in solitude in this way. I discovered that stillness and solitude aren't at all scary, and this realization made me feel most alive. I experience something exquisite in my aloneness, whereby I'm alone and yet never lonely. The reason is that my soul is my best friend.

These periods of non-action are heaven on earth to me. In the beginning, as I learned this rhythm of non-action/action, I questioned what I had accomplished on a given day. Eventually I came to understand I had just gone to the moon and back. Cultivating a rich inner world—a deep friendship and enduring love for my own soul—will perhaps be my greatest lifetime accomplishment.

In the Chicago area, I favor certain beaches. One in particular I love because it carries a distinct vibe of "being" rather than "doing." People walk more slowly, look around more, visit with one another, and generally appear quieter; whereas in my town, a mere eight miles away, the busyness vibe is often more palpable, even during seeming downtimes. The fast walking and talking with a friend, the social dog beach, the exercising, even the coffee klatch—while all good ways to spend time—feel more about doing than being.

Stillness of being can occur both within and without perceived busyness. The mind can be still, totally present, whether we are engaged in action or non-action. In other words, we can be "unbusy" even in the midst of seeming chaos. Stillness isn't so much about sitting still as it's about inner calm.

Having said this, I confess that after a big fortieth birthday weekend a few years back with lots of activity and social interaction, I realized how much I missed *myself* during the extravaganza. Similarly, my middle daughter explained at the age of eleven that she hadn't enjoyed her three weeks at an all-girls' summer camp because there wasn't sufficient alone time. I also realized after having many guests over for a dinner party that I had spent so much time focused on the "doing" aspects of the event that I didn't open my heart to sit, listen, and connect with my guests. Today I recognize that a conscious balance between doing and being, action and non-action, busyness and stillness, may be one of our highest offerings to ourselves and to the world at large.

A Moment of Silence in Our Schools

Many educational systems have recently enacted laws to enforce a moment of silence at the beginning of each school day. Whether we agree or disagree with these laws, once a decision has been made the question becomes how we can use it for our further development. I suggest perceiving the moment of silence in our schools not as a religious event, but as a powerful pause—a way of encouraging children to infuse moments of stillness and deeper connection to self into their day, whereby they take a few deep breaths, stop doing, and quiet the mind and the mouth. The benefits of meditation, whether standing quietly in a classroom or sitting yogi style on a mat, are plentiful.

As for those who feel that classrooms should be off and running from task to task at the onset of each day, it's worth bearing in mind that a number of famous individuals, including Einstein, encouraged simply *being* with a problem or an idea and *allowing* the creative answer to appear. It can be beneficial to forego constant mind chatter—the never-ending analytical, and often judgmental, twirl. By so doing, we get out of our own way.

Another Costco Run: Necessary or Superfluous?

Are your weeks filled to the brim? Is "I'm just so busy" a common utterance for you? Do you ever leave yet another meeting feeling unfulfilled? If the answer is a resounding yes, you're not alone. In the modern world, many of us seem to be drowning in our own busyness.

While there may have been a time that a Costco run was a necessary aspect of each week, when looked at from a different perspective we may find that the rewards no longer match the effort, making one-stop shopping worth the few extra dollars. Likewise, certain daily routines may have been a perfect fit while the kids were in preschool, while not as empowering now, when we yearn to start our own business and post-breakfast is when our best ideas typically flow. In other words, we need to ask ourselves whether our priorities are aligned with our overall soul purpose, or whether we're wasting precious hours each week in a time-suck of our own design.

Beyond even a full week of work, for most of us there are many hours of free time. Maybe we should think back to earlier days in kindergarten and take a hint. We would never have unnecessarily chosen hours pursuing no longer useful endeavors rather than building our dream house with blocks, painting our personal version of water lilies, or singing in our highest alto voice. The lesson in this is that beyond basic practicalities, busyness isn't so much something that happens to us as something we generate. The call is to *own* our busyness. Perhaps we can do more with our time than those who claim non-stop busyness. It's our choice: a rushed errand along with a quick stop at Starbucks during a much-needed lunch hour; or thirty minutes of soul time on a beautiful spring day? No right or wrong per se. Just a reminder that busyness itself isn't necessarily the villain, but our self-induced victimhood.

Travel Sports: Passion or Business, Democracy or Dictatorship?

Travel sports, mentioned earlier in connection with our son's broken wrist, have occasioned much discussion around busyness in our home. On the one hand we're delighted that two of our three children have participated in what many around the country, not to mention the world, consider a luxury. On the other hand, I often contemplate the point of it all.

The soul perspective is that there are multiple valid perspectives. No doubt much joy and personal development accompany competitive sports. They are an opportunity to experience what it means to prioritize, commit, and focus. I see this firsthand in my husband's work as a high school coach, in my children's desire to express themselves on the field, and through long discussions with my father-in-law, whom I mentioned earlier was a former professional baseball player. So I write as someone who isn't totally resistant to the culture of sports that's so deeply embedded in our society.

As the club mentality has spread over the past decade, it may be time to re-evaluate some of its facets. Although my children for the most part enjoyed the experience, deriving physical, emotional, and social empowerment from it, as a parent I sometimes felt like a sheep in a herd at the mercy of others, disempowered by a system that dictates so much of how our family time is spent, as well as how we use our finances. I found myself questioning the need to invest so much of our family time en route to yet another far away game.

Often parents and children find themselves afraid to speak up in a sports club for fear of repercussions for the child. My voice seeks to activate greater freedom and soul nourishment surrounding sports in our lives, particularly in the area of travel sports. Yet even the lower levels require a sizable commitment. I don't wish to throw the baby out with the bathwater, only to foster a travel sports environment that bears in mind the reason for its inception: children with a passion for the sport.

While some parents wish to make a name for their team, acquire a college scholarship for their child, and travel far and wide regardless of cost or the fracturing of family time, others feel that travel sports don't necessarily have to be so "all or nothing." A little more transparency, a tad more choice, and an ounce more appreciation for balance in terms of the family would go a long way to creating a better experience for all. I realize the clubs are businesses with needs that have to be met. But might not more open dialogue concerning the realities for both the club and parents uncover creative ways to enhance the positives and reshape the negatives in a manner we can all agree on?

Downtime Equals a Creative "Yes"

More and more Americans, whose culture of intense focus on productivity has been both its boon *and* nemesis, are realizing that optimal creativity stems from regular periods of free-form mind wandering. Everything humans have ever made germinated in someone's imagination.

According to recent studies, during downtime the brain undergoes purposeful connective threading that creates a sense of self within our rich inner world. It's therefore imperative we give ourselves permission each day to allow the natural flow of consciousness that occurs at those moments when we feel the most guilt over our non-productivity.

My creative insights and spiritual perceptions typically arise when I allow myself to relax into my daily tasks or chosen downtime. It's *always* when I'm at my least productive that intuitive flashes find space to flourish. Folding loads of laundry, blow-drying my hair, riding my bike, or staring out the window at a cardinal all provide the pause that sets my creative juices flowing. I now know why monks learned to relish scrubbing another floor, since the wandering mind offers spiritual sustenance and inspiration.

Martha and Mary: Two Sisters, Two Perspectives

I'm not a religious gal, and the Bible isn't a book I'm terribly familiar with. However, the story of Martha and Mary is one of the few that stuck with me from my upbringing. While traveling, Jesus stops at the home of these two sisters and their brother Lazarus. Martha, the older sister, immediately heads to the kitchen to take care of the physical details of his visit—food, plates, beverages, linens, and so on. Mary, the younger sister, offers him a chair and sits down to listen to what he has to say. Eventually Martha asks Jesus why he hasn't sent Mary to assist her in the kitchen, and he lovingly explains that Mary has made the better choice.

It's easy to empathize with Martha, especially at times such as the holidays when there's so much to do as we gather with loved ones and friends. Someone has to be the Martha, since gathering with others usually involves food and drink at the very least. Some truly enjoy this role. But in light of Jesus' words, might it be possible to host *simply,* so that we may also spend quality time with our visitors?

If you are a Mary—a category into which my mom and I both fall naturally—it's important to appreciate those who are more concerned with the physical aspects of a gathering, offering to assist in a way that feels genuine and helpful. This might mean making a simple pot of soup, setting the table, or helping serve dinner and clean up.

The point I take from the story is that we don't want to turn a role into an identity, which is what I suspect Jesus was pointing out to Martha. As a woman, she felt her sister ought to be busy in the kitchen with her, when they really needed a more balanced approach that included listening to the teaching. As Jesus put it, "Martha, Martha, you are worried and upset about many things, but few things are needed—or indeed only one. Mary has chosen what is better, and it will not be taken away from her."

Eventually, so much of what we always thought mattered feels tiresome and superfluous. It had its day before we even knew. When the outer drops away, we are left with one very precious life.

SHIFT

#6

From Hiding to Self-Expression

FROM RESTRAINT TO FREEDOM
FROM HOLDING BACK TO VULNERABILITY
FROM MASKS TO AUTHENTICITY
FROM FEAR TO COURAGE
FROM IMPOSED ARENAS TO NATURAL GATEWAYS
FROM EGO NEEDS TO SOUL PREFERENCES

Promise me you will not spend so much time treading water and trying to keep your head above the waves that you forget, truly forget, how much you have always loved to swim.
TYLER KNOTT GREGSON

Life invites us to begin the process of living true, finding within us the courage to stand in the fire of our soul's longings without guilt or shame for simply being ourselves. Slowly our restraint, our masks, our fears, the ways in which we hide, and the arenas we restrict ourselves to for self-expression dissipate.

As getting to know our soul facilitates a new comfort level within our own skin, we experience joyful self-expression. We discover what lights us up, makes our eyes sparkle, encourages our lips to smile, quickens our step, and generally causes us to shine both within and without.

The self-exploratory journey has two arms: shadow work and joyful self-expression. Although the two go hand in hand, and a certain joy accompanies even shadow work, for me the expressive aspect of self-exploration is more fun than dealing with my shadow. However, I know that for some it's more daunting, at least in the beginning.

On my path to wholeness, I actually flipped the model, as some do. After being broken open at age nineteen following my parents' divorce, I fell in love with the spiritual path, focusing for many years on knowing myself as soul rather than on the shadow aspects of myself. Eventually I had to acknowledge my shadow, which was initially tough since I loved the light aspects of awakening. But whichever route we take to awakening, the goal is to be able to express ourselves in all our glory.

I vividly remember watching two ducks in the water from a beach near my home in Chicago. I relished their lack of ego as they dove under again and again, their down butts and skinny legs sticking straight up. Without a care in the world, they kept lifting those butts. The freedom of it moved me, and I felt a desire to become soul naked. In that moment, I knew that nature in the form of trees, animals, and plants—together with my immediate surroundings, such as houses, buildings, and cars—was going to help me live true. If the duck could flash its butt, the mighty oak could stand tall, and my house could stand proud to be called a home, I could be Annie in her truest form. From this observation of the ducks, which might seem almost a non-event, a shift was born.

A key aspect of this shift is being self-loving enough to identify our own natural gateways—the ways in which we feel most connected to our soul, and therefore to the oneness—then having the courage to allow those gateways to open, so that we pass confidently through them to bloom and flourish.

We begin birthing our inner truth in ways that are unique to us, as we recognize that we no longer need to play it safe—no longer need to take care not to offend others by being ourselves. As we joyfully express ourselves, we want this for others. By exploring our natural gateways, it turns out we energetically give others permission to do the same, especially those closest to us who observe, and more importantly feel, the empowerment that comes with living from soul.

This empowerment stems from separating ourselves from what others are doing and instead taking small steps that honor who we are and where we are, allowing the whole world to see. Our true being comes out to play without apology. There are no words for this type of freedom.

Most of us were taught early on by others, especially well-meaning parents, that living true is unsafe. Consequently we learned to look away from our natural gateways, choosing some other direction. As a middle-aged woman, I've come to better understand my natural gateways, seeing them as my soul preferences, and now have the self-love, boundaries, and courage to walk through them. None of us can know, but most likely I'm at the halfway point of this beautiful incarnation as Annie Burnside, and I choose to live it out as soul-directed as possible. By so doing, I hope to be an example for not only my own children but all who cross my path. In a sense, I feel my life's mission is to assist, encourage, and support others as they too fall in love with their own souls.

As we reflect on our natural gateways, we expand the awareness of who we are as soul, rather than as a role. The person we are lies beyond all roles. When we allow ourselves to think and feel beyond our roles, often the floodgates open and we are quite surprised to encounter what comes to the fore as we move into self-expression.

Discover Your Gateways to Self-Expression

As a soul nurturer, I'm frequently asked, "How do I find my life's purpose? Please, give me some practical steps." My response is that there are unlimited pathways to self-expression and we must take those that are unique to *us*. I can however share a few tenets that have helped to move me in the direction of the self-expression I desire.

Natural gateways are the primary ways our soul opens to a connection felt with the oneness. These are of utmost importance to understand, both in terms of our personal development and offering our soul's purpose to the world. They will be the means through which we ultimately become the clearest possible channel for oneness on the relative plane. While rarely discussed in our current educational models, identifying and allowing natural gateways to be cultivated as young as possible would be a great service to humanity. This is especially the case given that our gateways are typically apparent in early childhood as the most natural way we feel "at home" with ourselves. There's often more than one, but usually not more than a handful.

To identify our gateways, we can ask a variety of questions such as: Where, how, and when does my soul feel most enlivened? Where, how, and when do I feel the greatest ease and flow? What do I know to be the truest aspect of myself? Which direction lights me up from deep within, firing me with a passion to move outward? How is peace enhanced within me? What allows for the greatest possibility of presence? The answers to these questions will provide important clues to our truth, source of inspiration, and joy—all states of being that allow our authentic self to shine forth from the inside out.

For me, one of the keys to uncovering my gateways was to identify where and when I most resembled a kid in a candy shop. Ideally, this "high" feeling becomes integrated not only into your favorite pastime, but also into your chosen career as you seek to make the "unofficial" official—although I need to state that making it official in this way isn't necessary and doesn't happen for everyone. Sometimes the natural gateways remain as the way we choose to spend our free time, also an essential aspect of wholeness.

Over twenty years ago, I was like a kid in a candy shop whenever I entered a metaphysical bookstore or the metaphysical section of a bookstore or library. I experienced elevated energy, my eyes sparkled, and my sense of joy intensified. Today I'm a soul nurturer and author, speaking, teaching, and writing on the very topics that have been my passion for more than two decades.

Thirty years ago, my husband was overjoyed each summer as he headed up to Wisconsin to counsel, teach, and coach lively boys at a camp for eight weeks. Like a kid in a candy shop, he came alive during his interactions with eager and enthusiastic youth in their teachable moments. Fast forward to today, and he has been teaching and coaching at a local high school for more than two decades, truly living the soul calling he felt early in his development.

Ask yourself: What's my candy shop? Cull the aspects of it you love. Analyze the various facets of your joy. Brainstorm viable ideas and create something new from the inspiration.

As you go about this, make sure self-care becomes the most important aspect of your life, since our personal state of being has tremendous power to shape our reality. The profound recognition that *who you are as a person* has a huge impact on whatever you will accomplish, inevitably requires that self-care be your top priority. Your internal reality is the source of your external self-expression, rather than a mere effect of it. Your inner world is running the show. For this reason, balance and your inner well-being come first.

Other Gateways

Beginning at the age of four, I found I love to dance. It was a vital aspect of my early years and the primary way in which I joyfully self-expressed. Dance and all kinds of music remain two of my main gateways in terms of connecting with the oneness via my soul. Music in particular is something I utilize daily.

As a child, writing was also of great value to my soul as a means of expressing my truth, more so than speaking. In my adult years I've filled many journals that I call *The Voice of My Soul*. I also blog, write articles and books, send prolific emails and texts, and generally express the inner linings of my soul most easily through writing. It's a natural gateway for me.

Although the whole of nature speaks to me, water feeds my soul like no other natural element. As I've grown older, I've found myself drawn to it more frequently, even daily in the warmer months, as a means of inner sustenance. Sometimes I swim or walk by the water, though it's the energetic connection to my own soul that I seek.

Walking and biking alone, beneath a brilliant sun, often create within me a soul expansion that rises upward and outward through my chest in bursts of gratitude. There really are no words for the natural gateway that these two pursuits offer. In a most grounded way, I know myself as a blended being, whereby my inner awareness of soul facilitates embracing totally my external reality. The feeling of immersing myself in every aspect of life unreservedly is one of my greatest joys.

My children, as all children will, revealed their natural gateways to us at an early age. Our older daughter is a deep thinker with a propensity for humanitarianism, diplomacy, and international relations. Our younger daughter is noncompetitive and most alive with animals and assisting others who may be marginalized by mainstream society in some way, be it the elderly or those with different abilities. As already described, our son has shown exceptional fluidity in his physicality from the earliest of ages, and hence athletics is one of his most natural gateways. Of course, each of our children is a whole being with several gateways, but these were all detected early on and have remained a large aspect of their self-expression in ways that highlight the oneness expressed in their humanness.

A large part of what I do as a parent, friend, and soul nurturer is to assist others in identifying their natural gateways and encouraging, supporting, and giving them permission through my own example to walk through these gateways without guilt or apology. One of my joys is to witness another own the inner light that desires its due, as all birthrights do.

Beyond myself and my own family, through my work I've come across several beautiful examples of natural gateways, a few of which I want to share with you. For instance, I think of a boy who loved fabrics, clothes, and different textures from an early age. He was extremely tactile, so that caressing a silk scarf was the type of thing that felt ecstatic to his soul. Upon turning twelve, his mother, who had observed her son carefully through the years, gave him a sewing machine for his birthday. This was the finest gift he had ever received. Through this act of acceptance of her child, her son knew that he was seen, heard, and acknowledged.

A young girl simply adored playing in dirt with plants and all things garden. Through the years, her mother encouraged her botanic inclination. When it came time to apply to college, despite being from a well-to-do family whose members typically attended well-known universities, this mother honored her daughter's natural gateway, helping her relocate to a part of the country where she could practice her love of gardening. Fast-forward several years, and the daughter heads her own large greenhouse business.

While observing a man playing his guitar and singing with his eyes closed, as the music became more and more passionate, I felt in my soul the truth of this individual's natural self-expression. Tears sprung to my eyes as I realized, not with my mind but through a feeling of oneness, that this man had entered his natural gateway. His performance in an old bluesy type bar moved me.

To foster the pursuit of natural gateways in our fellow humans is one of the greatest offerings we can give another. It says, "I see you. I love you. Come as you are." Do we allow ourselves and our fellow blended beings this level of individuality, which ironically leads to a natural feeling of and deepened understanding of oneness? Do we encourage one another to live true, from soul rather than role?

In short, are we willing to stop hiding and become soul naked in order to live true? Our power lies in our natural gateways. When it comes to personal truth, don't ever allow others to rain on your internal parade. Listen to your own soul, deferring to no one in this regard. Our special soul pursuits are embedded in our DNA, and they are ours to express in any way that feels the most natural.

Allow your gateways to unfold organically in divine time; for they require no force to emerge, only acknowledgment, encouragement, and love. As you enter *your* candy shop, be sure to enjoy all the deliciousness that awaits you.

A Further Way Facebook Helped Me

I talked earlier about how I was relatively slow getting on Facebook. Now, as I look back over the past few years, I see that it's been like a giant playground for me to experience being more forthrightly myself. Through it, I've increasingly owned and used my precious voice.

As a result of the way I grew up pleasing people, I flew under the radar as far as expressing my true voice. I remember not wanting the focus to be on me. I always wanted my turn to share to be short and sweet. I felt the same way on Facebook at first, always wondering what I had to offer that others wanted to hear. But after several years, not anymore.

It was through Facebook that I initially became aware of an aspect of my shadow that I call *diminishment by comparison*. Every now and then she would appear when I noticed others be successful, especially those in a similar field or experiencing something close to my heart; each time I felt "less than." Facebook has allowed me to befriend this part of my shadow and really get to know her. I call her Diminishment Donna, and I can't tell you how much headway I've made in freeing myself from the comparison game through Facebook.

Facebook has assisted me in being truly happy for others, allowing me to participate in their successes, setbacks, challenges, and joys. The daily practice of acknowledging others with a comment or a thumbs up has freed me from the insidious noose, "If I acknowledge your success, I somehow diminish myself."

As a soul nurturer, I need to network. It's simply not possible to be a communicator, a writer, and an empathizer who connects with others emotionally without networking. However, since I tend more to the introvert lane, networking via local golf outings, gala events, power lunches, and cocktail parties isn't my natural way. This is where Facebook has been enormously valuable. Facebook has allowed me to impact others virtually, simultaneously enriching my life with a cadre of friends. While some claim that cyber friendships aren't the "real" kind, I disagree. I share much depth and true soul sisterhood with both women and men on Facebook, having found a soul tribe that sees and uplifts me—and I them.

I used to journal solely for my own personal development. Facebook afforded me the opportunity to share my insights on life's experiences so that others could benefit from my inner work should they wish to do so, and vice versa. In our modern world, there often simply isn't the sharing and mirroring that was available to us more directly within our own communities in earlier times. Facebook can be the new village in this regard, and I use it purposefully and gratefully.

Another bonus of being on Facebook is that it has offered a multigenerational venue for interaction among my daughters, their peers, and myself. When I was a teen, I certainly never knew the inner thoughts of my friends' mothers. I had no idea beyond what I may have observed and intuited who they were as human beings when they weren't in the role of "mom." To connect with different generations is something I cherish, with the advantages going both ways as we offer one another mutually empowering insights from our personal truth.

I also value being part of a large and diverse group of bloggers, which on a daily basis teaches me so much about the sharing of ideas. For someone who is self-employed and works primarily alone, this serves as a touchstone to the humanity of others. Reading their blogs, interacting on a variety of topics, and learning how to respond to negative comments and stay inspired as a writer has taught me much about myself and others, broadening my perspective. Every day I encounter something of value to chew on.

When it comes to the courage to live true and share "Annieness" with the world, Facebook has been like twenty years' worth of personal growth in a short space. Had someone told me a few years back that I would be sharing regularly from my soul for all the world to see, I wouldn't have believed them. Being more fully myself on Facebook paved the way for me to be more fully myself in all other areas of my life, a blessing beyond blessings for a gal who used to feel most comfortable hiding her soul.

Choose You!

Riding my bike into the city of Chicago, I paused to rest, relax, and reflect at one of my favorite spots overlooking Lake Michigan. It's a place where there's a bird sanctuary. When stopping at this spot, I often use the time to contemplate world affairs and the nature of reality; however, on this occasion I found myself reflecting instead on what I truly enjoy as Annie the blended being—not Annie the mom, wife, woman, soul nurturer, friend, or American, but simply Annie. As the floodgates opened, I found myself immersed in a celebration of all things Annie, which occasioned a sense of self-love and acceptance.

The time is *now* to know ourselves better and to choose what we truly prefer as often as possible. We have infinitely more choices in both our daily living and future direction than most of us are willing to admit to ourselves. I'm not talking about just the big decisions in life, but all the little things.

To illustrate from my own preferences as they occurred to me on that bike ride, I prefer pizza and beer over champagne and pate, being over doing, open field over amusement park, bike over car, porch swing over roller coaster, convertible over SUV, park bench over shopping, beach over desert, urban living over country, old and rehabbed over new construction, happy hour over late night, soul over classical, blues over jazz, paddle boarding over water skiing, pontoon over speedboat, brownstone over high rise, NBA over NFL, water over mountains, meadow over forest, open windows over AC, public park over country club, live music over DJ, Al Fresco dining over indoor seating, charitable donations over political giving, coffee over tea, less over more, simple over busy, direct connect over religion, diversity over homogeneity, driving over flying, picnic over fine dining, early riser over night owl, medical intuitive over traditional doctor, book over movie, outdoor exercise over gym, deep over superficial, pancakes over waffles, bikini over one-piece, flip flops over high heels, newspaper over magazine, people watching over museum, walking over running, diner over chain, local over mall, late afternoon sun over mid-morning sun.

While many of my preferences may involve frivolous matters, they represent the keys to the castle—the inner one. I share them with you only to provoke you to become more aware of your *own* preferences. The time is now to know our soul better. If not now, then when? It's up to each soul to captain their own ship, and yet many of us don't even allow our soul to serve as first mate.

Jason Collins' Announcement Was Family Discussion Gold

The machismo on the sports fields across America and beyond remains one of the strongholds of a patriarchal paradigm that shapes much in our world. That stronghold was weakened when Jason Collins came out as gay, a topic we discussed with our children, covering sexuality, equality, and labeling. We talked about how what our culture tends to deem "manly" and "feminine" can affect our courage to live true.

I don't think we can underestimate the power of our cultural institutions—celebrity and sports being the big two in America. To uplift our world, we need dominant players on our cultural landscape to help usher in a change of heart, embracing peace, acceptance, unity, and a love of people of every type.

As part of our discussion about Jason Collins, we read aloud tweets from different individuals our children respect in the sports world and beyond, both supportive and intolerant, explaining that it's also important to accept those who are intolerant. If we truly believe there are countless paths up the mountain, we must include as a path those who believe there's only one path. Of all the aspects of the Jason story we covered, this last one was the hardest for our children to understand.

Most of all, it's the freedom—the escape from hiding and shame—that we wanted our children to understand, so that they know they'll be supported in their wholeness and truth, whatever that may in due course look like for them, straight or gay. For me, it felt like a watershed moment. I could see and feel in their eyes a sense of relief and empowerment from knowing that, in every aspect of their lives, they can be unapologetically true to themselves. Thanks in part to the many who will now go before them, they have a greater sense of safety that they can offer their gifts *and* be fully themselves.

Ram Dass and the Lady with the Fruit Hat

During a radio show interview for my first book, the host shared the story of an occurrence at a Ram Dass lecture. In the late 1960s, the Harvard psychologist and psychedelic explorer, most famous for his book *Be Here Now*, went to India where he became a spiritual teacher following his foray into the paranormal through LSD experiences with Dr. Timothy Leary. As the story goes, he was giving a lecture to a large group explaining his early LSD trips and how absolutely otherworldly they were, including a description of his magnificent nirvanic experiences in India post drugs.

Throughout the lecture, an elderly woman near the front, wearing a hat topped with plastic fruit, nodded in agreement. Out of all the hundreds present, Ram Dass couldn't help but notice this woman who was so spellbound by his descriptions of drug-induced and shamanic-induced bliss trips. After the lecture, he sought out this most enchanting woman and asked her why she had nodded and grinned from ear-to-ear throughout his talk. Had she experimented with mind-altering drugs or travelled to India to study in ashrams under the tutelage of a guru?

The woman smiled and said that indeed she hadn't. Likely someone's beloved grandmother, she undoubtedly hadn't been of the age to experience the 60s as a free spirited hippie. Then with a sparkle in her eyes she said, "I crochet."

It was Ram Dass' turn to smile. This dear and quite elderly woman, who had probably never even heard of most of the metaphysical teachings Ram Dass shared in his lecture, offered one of the great truths that crosses all boundaries. There are an infinite number of streams to the glorious sea. Follow the ones that are unique to you. Feel your *own* way, because the ecstasy that so many spiritual masters speak of is available to each and every one of us when we come to know our own soul. Let the simple answer "I crochet" be your guiding example of living true.

SHIFT

#7

From Striving to Contentment

From Trying to Simply Breathing
From Struggle to Relaxation
From Holding On to Letting Go
From Attachment to Surrender
From Planned Strategies to Organic Growth
From Project Motivation to Soul Calling
From Needing a Timetable to Trusting the Process
From Long-term Goals to Spontaneity

He turned around and began climbing down the huge pillar of other caterpillars. This time he didn't curl up. He stretched out full length and looked straight into the eyes of each one. He marveled at the variety and beauty, amazed that he had never noticed it before. He whispered to each, 'I've been up; there's nothing there.' Most paid no attention; they were too intent on climbing. He realized how he had misread the instinct to get high. To get to the 'top' he must fly not climb.
Trina Paulus

Many feel that if we give up striving, we won't accomplish anything. From my perspective, this couldn't be further from the truth. When I speak of "striving," I'm referring to an underlying energy that creates anxiety, unrest, and a lack of flow—the opposite of contentment. If we spend our lives striving for the next moment rather than basking in the organic unfolding of our own life lived, contentment will remain forever out of reach.

Productivity doesn't have to be at the expense of contentment. When we let go of striving, we continue to hold a vision—continue to change and grow and learn and try. It just feels so different. The paradox of "everything has meaning" and "nothing really matters" comes into play. As a blended being, both perspectives hold true simultaneously.

It's a change of input that's called for with this shift, not necessarily a change of output. Practical plans of both the short-term and long-term variety are still made, but the energy comes from a different source. We become task-specific rather than strategic, allowing focus and action to rise and fall one task at a time. Being task-specific is a totally different way to move through a day—a life. It flips on its head the traditional energy thread of always striving. We still work hard. It's just that our focus is more on organic growth and trusting the process rather than on goals, projections, and timetables.

Contentment, Numbers, and the Big Arena

At the beginning of a recent summer, I felt quite tired. Not hard-physical-labor-fifty-weeks-a-year tired. Not single-parent tired. Not grieving-for-the-loss-of-a-loved-one tired. But nonetheless emotionally, mentally, and spiritually tired. My eyes began to feel strained and ache. This was the first sign that a shift in perspective was about to be integrated.

When I started out on my current career nine years ago, I imagined my professional trajectory being similar to the many New Age spiritual authors I'd read. Write a book, create a brand, gain a following, and eventually enter the big arena. Author Brene Brown remarks that it takes great courage to step into the arena. But during this particular summer, a nagging feeling I'd stuffed down for years began to surface—the feeling that it also takes great courage to step out of the arena once inside. As I pondered this, a further insight came to me: it takes courage not to enter the arena in the first place.

The question I now faced was a simple one. What did I want? For in each of these scenarios the variable was *me*.

I've never been Type A about my work, the arena, or anything in my life for that matter. I'm simply not wired that way. Nevertheless, there was a striving—a "not there yet"—simmering beneath not only my work but my life. I had invested several years in trying to get my name out to the wider public. In fact, right before this life-changing summer, I had engaged in two major attempts to leap into bigger arenas, both of which resulted in a fairly large amount of money spent and the feeling that it was "all wrong" for me. The result was that I lost my motivation to be in the arena—any arena, other than that of my own soul.

At first I gave this shift much thought, before eventually choosing to let it be. I took the entire summer off to be with my family and enjoy life as it was. As the summer unfolded, I listened—not to the outside world, and not to the big players in my field, but to my own soul. What I was listening for was this: at forty-three, what did I, Annie Burnside, truly desire from my work and from my life? I asked this question in full knowing that I had the capacity to choose whatever the answer might be.

Turns out, when I took away the outside aspects of creating a brand—numbers, readership, statistics, pulling, pushing, climbing, higher earning power, constant need for more publicity, and all else under the umbrella of "success," I enjoy my chosen work, but not at the expense of "Annieness." I realized I was basically a content person and always had been. It's why I don't like long-term goals, don't do yearly plans, don't thrive on wearing many hats all at once. Multitasking drains me rather than energizes me.

By the end of that summer, the word "contentment"—and more importantly, the *feeling* of contentment—overtook me. I came to understand that for me, the climb into the arena might just be a big race to nowhere. I also realized with great relief that I'm more than okay with never getting there. I knew without a doubt and with utter delight that my soul was grinning from ear to ear. I see now that the big arena is my own life lived in alignment with soul. The soul arena is as big as it gets. The climb is actually an inward journey, not external. And I am already there. We all are.

This clarity that had been germinating all summer rushed in full-on one sunny afternoon in late August in the form of an ecstatic "knowing" while driving my daughter and listening to Sheryl Crow's song *Easy*.

When all the striving is over, it is indeed easy.

Tiger Mom Meets Butterfly Mom

Can you take one more dissection of the Tiger Mom phenomenon that took the nation, even the world, by storm? She is in the news with a second book that expands on the premise of the first, once again igniting heated discussions on parenting. I believe that the tiger mom and most all parents, no matter what their parenting stripes, love their children and desire the best for them. But I see them as parenting from what they believe about *themselves*.

To me, the key point of distinction in this debate is one's definition of success. Is success primarily about status, financial gain, and intellectual achievement stemming from a "survival of the fittest" paradigm? As a butterfly mom, I hold a much different view of success. From a butterfly mom's perspective, success is much more about a child's metamorphosis from a beautiful, divine caterpillar—perfect already in every way despite any outward appearances to the contrary—into a conscious global citizen who knows their own heart. The main difference between the tiger mom and the butterfly mom is an internal focus rather than external. In the heart of the butterfly mom, there exists a high regard for both soul evolution and self-realization.

While I can't speak for the tiger mom, I know that the butterfly mom's deepest desire for her children is the ability to live true, courageously, and comfortably within their own skins. Her parenting role will feel most complete if her children become capable of holding their heads high *as she is*. Such children radiate a love of self and others. Fostering authenticity, which involves being liberated to live one's soul purpose, is the ultimate gift a butterfly mom offers her child. Seeing, hearing, and acknowledging her children moment by moment, day by day, and soul to soul is by far her greatest parenting achievement.

In this parenting paradigm, a parent would *much* prefer to see her child become a lawn-care worker if the child most enjoys nature, an artist if the child's inner well of creativity is bountiful, or a salesperson if an extroverted tendency is strong, than to make a choice for what the world deems "success" for the sake of pleasing the parents or gaining the approval of society. To "know thyself" and offer one's uniqueness to the world is what the butterfly mom hopes to model and support.

This doesn't mean children shouldn't be encouraged to try their best in school, try new experiences, or stick with things when the going gets difficult. Neither does it mean handing over the parenting reins in any way. It's just that when we parent from soul rather than role, we foster qualities such as joy, love, compassion, empowerment, gratitude, freedom, and intimacy. We impart the highest regard for the voice of one's own soul, which means we enjoy seeing our children dance, paint, bake, sing, play, laugh, and socialize joyfully right alongside the academics, the music lessons, and the ballet classes.

I would rather see my child dance in ecstasy, expressing with every cell in her body who she *really* is as an eternal, infinite, creative being, than see her stick to the "right" path because she feels as if it *should* be a fit regardless of personal preference. I recognize that passionately strumming a guitar in the blessed interior space of direct divine connection is viewed as just as purposeful and important as a future walk through the halls of a famed academic institution. In a nutshell, I would rather help my child identify and harness her gifts to create a life that reflects her soul than see her focus on a pathway to a high-powered career that may not resonate.

As tiger moms meet butterfly moms, perhaps we can appreciate the numerous common threads to be found in our mutual love for our children. As parents, we wouldn't even be interested in the recent dialogue over the book if this weren't the soul's cry. A balance between the being and the doing, the busyness and the stillness, the norms of society and the individual passions, the focused eye of the tiger and the fluttering wing of the butterfly, may be an important bridge for all to cross in our era of change and opportunity.

Weight Loss, Maintenance, and Joy

Maintaining *our* unique, natural body weight—a continuous process for most, and for many a lifelong thread of anxiety and a loathsome burden—can be viewed in a new light when we come from the contentment that accompanies soul rather than role.

Through my years on the spiritual journey *and* in a

weight maintenance mindset, about ten years ago I discovered that the two readily go hand in hand and can be especially powerful when consciously acknowledged and integrated. The more I cleaned out my psychic debris, the more aware I became that my interior is absolutely and unequivocally running the show, determining *even* the end result of the forbidden chocolate cake. Our state of being—the energy that lies beneath the surface of all we think, say, and do—is the source of the end manifestation that becomes our reality.

While healthy eating habits and exercise are beneficial, just as important is our state of being while consuming food, engaging in physical activity, and moving through the day. We are energy beings first and foremost. For many this is a missing piece in all aspects of life, including issues with weight.

As so many experts have begun to teach us, emotional baggage—detrimental energy carried within the whole being—must be owned and navigated so that lasting change can occur. Once freed from the past, the freedom to move *up* the emotional scale towards appreciation, joy, and empowerment increases, opening the way for maintenance of an optimal weight.

Eating one Oreo in an authentic state of peace, love, and gratitude towards *ourselves* is far healthier than dining on a salad in a state of anger and resentment. Likewise, running a marathon with a long-held belief in "not being enough" may be more detrimental than sitting on a park bench day after day in a state of neutrality and calm. A variety of factors affect our health and longevity beyond genetics, our state of mind being one of them. Perhaps this is why there are so many stories of happy and content individuals who live to be a hundred or more while eating bacon and eggs every morning and imbibing whiskey in the evenings.

I'm not advocating the adoption of unhealthy practices.

Wholesome food and an active life are always the highest choice for the physical body. I'm simply inviting a heightened consciousness with regard to what occurs energetically in all that we think, say, and do. The inner world holds the key to all we seek to be.

SHIFT

#8

From Back End Awareness to Front End Awareness

FROM BLAME TO ACCOUNTABILITY
FROM UNCONSCIOUSNESS TO PRESENCE
FROM RANDOMNESS TO MINDFULNESS
FROM RIGIDITY TO FLOW
FROM LACK OF DISCRIMINATION TO DISCERNMENT
FROM REACTING TO REALITY TO CREATING REALITY
FROM COINCIDENCE TO SYNCHRONICITY

We already have everything we need. There is no need for self-improvement. All these trips that we lay on ourselves—the heavy duty fearing that we're bad and hoping that we're good, the identities that we so dearly cling to, the rage, the jealousy and the addictions of all kinds—never touch our basic wealth. They are like clouds that temporarily block the sun. But all the time our warmth and brilliance are right here. This is who we really are. We are one blink of an eye away from being fully awake.
PEMA CHODRON

Front end responsibility *creates* reality while back end pedaling *reacts* to it. Learning to factor myself in at all times through front end awareness and setting boundaries rather than waiting until the back end of an interaction, situation, or experience to clean up the debris made a huge difference in the quality of my life.

We generate much less suffering for ourselves by living true, speaking truth, and acting from our soul. All of these are front end ways of living that create few back end issues to be dealt with after the fact. From how we educate our children to how we live in a democracy, how we navigate family life, and how we seek a fulfilling career—all such choices when made from front end awareness alleviate much back end disharmony.

If we factor ourselves in on the front end, we have the opportunity in each of our experiences to determine who we are in relationship to it. Our job is to decide who we choose to be in relationship to anything and everything before it chooses us.

Sometimes I have difficulty seeing how I had a hand in creating a certain reality. This leads to uncovering aspects of energetic input and output that have been hidden from my conscious view. This type of inner work, which has to be performed once we are already stuck in the muck, with practice becomes integrated as foresight. No need to be hard on ourselves, only to move towards increased awareness.

To create the reality we desire on the front end without all of the dramatic layers, we must know ourselves more intimately—know our soul. This greater intimacy with soul requires not only focusing on our own energetic offerings, but also on what we allow to enter past our boundaries. When we contemplate the interactive process, we see the impossibility of creating anything from someone else's vantage point. We have zero choice in their offerings, as they are for them to choose, not us. We are only in control of our own. However, while we can't see through another's lens, as it's absolutely unique to them, we can expand our vantage point to consider their lens as part of the equation.

Van Morrison's song *Cleaning Windows* often comes to mind when I'm engaged in self-examination. The personal lens through which we perceive reality can be cleaned like a window when we make self-care a priority. We become aware of how, why, when, and where we choose to focus our energy. As we become more aware, we are empowered on the front end. Front end work is beneficial to all involved because as our boundaries become a priority and hopefully impenetrable, we create the space for honest exchanges. The idea is to become whole as early as possible in order to live our highest potential as parents, spouses, neighbors, supervisors, workers, and citizens.

Assessing Energy Upfront

Today I'm much better about assessing energy on the front end and choosing to either partake in it or to pass. When we choose not to join the dance, the energy stops in its tracks. It's then up to the person who initiated it to deal with it. In this way, we save ourselves a lot of back end work.

Before we either initiate an energy charge or react to one, it pays to ask ourselves whether what we're getting into is worth it. The more awakened we become, the more likely we are to smile and remain nonreactive in the face of either strong-arming or more passive forms of bullying. This type of energy emanates from *the other person's* psychic debris, not ours, so there's never a need to take it on. This front end energy assessment has changed my life. I now know it's my right to maintain neat borders when it comes to my energy field. I try to say "yes" only to energy that feels like a fit for my soul.

With this shift, I must add that my relationship with the oneness via my own soul has been of paramount importance. I know direct divine connection as my birthright, and I use it daily to assist me with inner work, including strong, self-loving boundaries. We don't need a reason, such as distress or pain, to embrace this connection. If we're tempted to react to a situation, all that's needed is to breathe and consciously become aware of this larger perspective. For a time we may move in and out of awareness of the oneness that's our true being, but with a little practice we find we no longer lose awareness. As this increasingly becomes the case, we rarely rush into an energy exchange that may wreak emotional havoc on the back end.

And here's a real surprise—at least it was for me. Once we learn how to protect ourselves with boundaries, we realize that boundaries are actually needed less and less!

When we consciously participate in creating our own reality, we notice aspects of reality that many others don't. For instance, we are aware of when something feels amiss, and we quickly determine where separation consciousness has crept in, obscuring our connection with the oneness. When we make a decision, we choose to make it a "right decision," though with an understanding there can't really be a wrong decision from the larger perspective, since the energy behind the decision will make the difference when it comes to the final outcome. We make choices from soul that lean in the direction of flow between our different roles, even if only by a few degrees.

When we consciously participate in creating our own reality, as we interact out in the world, our priority is to stay awake to the underlying energy via our sixth sense rather than simply relying on our five physical senses as our means of navigation. In other words, we make all our choices from soul, utilizing discernment over discrimination. We recognize that all options are part of the oneness, but that some are simply a higher choice *for us*.

Hence, whether we are making a choice that concerns

a more superficial matter or one that serves our deeper calling, we value mindfulness and intent. We recognize that interior leads to exterior, rather than the opposite, and understand what kind of energies best suit our own, then choose accordingly, saying "yes" only to those interactions—emails, appointments, meetings, friendships, financial deals, outings—that feel like a match. In this way we choose not to run ourselves ragged on the front end, only to reap the repercussions on the back end.

When we consciously participate in creating our own reality, the present moment is understood to be the most empowering consideration, with the understanding that appreciation for the now, coupled with enthusiasm for the future, creates an optimal space for well-being. We realize there's no perfect formula, and so we trust ourselves moment by moment.

True spiritual power stems from placing greater emphasis on all matters front end—both in terms of energetic healing and energetic assessment as needed—so that we're able to follow through with the physical action or non-action that best suits our soul. It's as simple and as complex as that.

How to Make Tuning In a Priority

When it comes to our children, knowledge of their inner compass—and, as important, *permission* to use it daily for both big and small decisions—is perhaps the most powerful tool we can offer. Even as babes rocking in our arms, we can whisper into their ears the truth of their divine heritage and all that this means for their well-being.

For many years now, in our home we have daily discussed, utilized, and cherished intuition. Our three teens have come to see that they do indeed have the capacity to hear the voice of their own soul, and we invite them to listen to it at every turn. Yes, we respect the rational mind as well; but in our family, even though it sometimes goes against the "shoulds" of societal norms, intuition reigns. It's a conscious choice on our part to lean in the intuitive direction when it comes to making a decision.

When faced with a decision as a family, if we need to search out information, we do it. If we need to seek help or advice, we do this as well. But ultimately we rely on our intuition to guide us in each step toward our final decision. It's important to get into the habit of identifying intuitions daily, until they become the natural means of navigating life.

We utilize five different ways to access our intuitive nature:

1) *Feel your way.* This is a reminder to get quiet for a moment and *feel* the choice that leads in a direction of increased peace, joy, ease, and flow. For instance, when our older daughter said she might want to give up playing soccer after nine years in the sport, we invited her to close her eyes and let us know how continuing to play on her high-level travel team felt, and how creating the space to try new things felt. Her answer was astounding. While continuing to play made her feel heavy and anxious, moving on felt like a weight was being lifted off her shoulders and made her smile. She had her answer.

2) *Be aware of vibes.* As blended beings we are able to pick up on the energy that surrounds us. My husband and I have taught our children that they are like radio receivers. We ask them to check in with the vibes around them regularly. They know that detecting vibes is a valuable resource, especially as their independence increases. When dropping them off for outings with friends or as they head out on their bikes, we often remind them to be aware of any vibes they might pick up, then evaluate them carefully to determine whether there's real danger or whether they are coming from irrational fear. Even when they receive positive vibes from a person or situation, we caution them

to be aware of the shadow. In short, we remind them to stay awake.

3) *Listen to your body.* The body provides a helpful navigational system, though it needs careful interpretation. We have held many family discussions to lay the groundwork for this understanding to become integrated in our children. People talk about getting a red light in a situation, or a gut feeling. It might take the form of lethargy, a headache, a stomachache, low energy, fatigue, a rash, an ailment, or any malady that comes on suddenly. It's important to evaluate whether such a red light or gut feeling is coming from real danger, or whether our past programming is causing us to doubt a path that's actually one we would do well to take. An invitation to broaden our experience of life and discover a new aspect of ourselves can feel just as threatening as a warning not to go down a particular road. Likewise, a green light in the form of excitement, enthusiasm, high energy, smiling, peace, a sparkle in the eye, butterflies, and an easing of previous physical symptoms or ailments can be both a positive intuition or a trap. Sex with someone totally inappropriate yet extremely enticing, drugs, and other harmful activities can all produce a high that can't be trusted. It's up to each of us to make the physical connection to our larger reality and discern the wise choice.

4) *Live true.* Authenticity is a priority in our family. We teach our children that the greatest gift they can offer themselves and the world at large is their truth. Intuition plays a big part in identifying our truth as we feel what resonates for us in all aspects of life. We stress again and again that there's so much more occurring than what meets the eye; and if they choose to allow it, they can uncover their own truth regardless of the dictates of society. As parents, showing them how to use their intuition goes a long way in helping them captain their ship.

5) *I love myself.* This reminder sits on our bathroom

mirror. Self-love is part of every choice in our family. Betrayal of self is much more insidious in our culture than many realize. We often get intuitive hits, creative ideas, and a resonance of truth, but choose not to follow them because of fear we'll disappoint others or let them down. We teach our children that following their truth will serve not only their highest good, but ultimately also the highest good of the other.

Time to Change the Way We Educate Our Children

For adults and older children, there's much back end work to be done with regard to psychic debris. But for our young, we must consider carefully the *front end* work of parenting, spiritual development, and education, in order to lessen the development of the shadow in our children in the first place. To accomplish this, we must change the way in which we educate children by completely *flipping* our current model of education.

For a start, we need to shift the financial resources for education from top-down to bottom-up. The earliest years of a child's life and education are the most important, as study after study has shown. All parents understand this on some level, and yet as a society we've refused to implement what we know. Teaching parents how to parent effectively, together with providing early education for our young, must become a financial priority. This doesn't necessarily mean more money flowing into the system, but rather allotting less at the top (university and high school levels) and more at the bottom (preschool and elementary, along with early parenting programs).

We need to revamp *what* we teach and *how* we teach in our schools, based on reevaluating what it means to be an educated world citizen. We need an educational system that stresses awareness *and* knowledge. It's not enough to continue teaching mere facts. We must offer a path to wisdom that takes into consideration a child's soul—something entirely different from religious dogma, which needs to be kept separate from public education.

We Must Go First

Who becomes the next president every four years, while important, is far less important than is each one of us individually, through our own personal development, moving on a path from an ego-based state to soul-based awareness.

In this 21st century, if we are to move forward as a species in a peaceful way, inner work has to step into the spotlight. It can't be restricted to those on a psychological or spiritual path of growth as it is now, but must become mainstream, a basic characteristic of the global culture. Only in this way will we see widespread changes in every aspect of society. Until then, no matter who our leaders are, we're simply applying band-aids to our problems.

In many ways, elections, while democratic and well-meaning in origin, mask the deeper issue of our interior worlds. It's for this reason I'd love to see a candidate stand up and announce, "I can't change *for* you what you can only change yourself from within." How refreshingly different that would be! We alone can release ourselves from an outdated perspective that no longer serves us either as individuals or collectively.

Imagine a world in which people lived free of psychic debris and in which their daily lives were like a kid in a candy shop. When a population becomes whole, problems get dealt with from the inside out.

The Dalai Lama Says, "The World Will Be Saved By the Western Woman"

What exactly did the Dalai Lama mean by his intuitive

assessment of the role of western women in the transformation of our world?

The work I do as a soul nurturer is right now primarily with western women, since they tend to be the ones who have the inclination, time, education, and relative affluence to self-explore. I find many women feel an underlying layer of guilt for having such an opportunity. Yet someone must go first if there's to be a large-scale awakening, and perhaps that someone is the western woman. Self-realization has moved far beyond monks on a mountaintop. Today spiritual awakening is occurring right here, right now in our neighborhoods, on the sidelines of little league games, and in our places of work.

The western woman holds the power to transform our world into a more peaceful, harmonious community that celebrates diversity. There are no limits to what women can contribute to all sectors of society from a more divinely feminine, intuitive way of being. A greater feeling of connection to all of life will spread through feminine compassion into our educational, political, economic, and healthcare systems. Of course, it goes without saying that no matter our gender, we all have both masculine and feminine energies, and women can help awaken the feminine in males.

Focus as a Tool

As I've heard many spiritual teachers say, *the energy flows where the attention goes.* Focus is a creative tool that leads to physical manifestation, generating a consistent and expanded energy flow that allows for greater access to inner wisdom.

Energy consciously directed toward a specific desired creation announces to the universe, loudly and clearly, a sense of purpose. I have found that when the divine connection is open and pulsating with purposeful energy, assistance from both the spiritual realm and earthly connections expands exponentially, providing more frequent intuitive flashes and divinely inspired synchronicities. However, this purposeful flow of energy is fundamentally different from what's often referred to as "setting an intention." This mental exercise often involves egoic thought, which has a "forced" feel, as if we have to make something happen. This isn't at all the same as the natural flow of soul. So be careful to watch for any *tension* in that word "intention" when you begin directing your energy toward a purpose.

Whenever we set a rigid intention, we move out of flow. With each need for a preferred singular outcome and the masks that we use to maneuver things to get it, we lose some of our soul's creative impetus—which is always aimed at serving the highest good for *all*—and resist the multifaceted outcome, often hidden yet available. To be passionate about the intricacies of our life *without* being attached to specific outcomes, while simultaneously living true within our own skin, is a sure sign of authentic power and spiritual mastery.

Look closely at your own expectations in all areas of your life. They will crop up each and every time you enter a new arena of choices. Most of us turn our preferences into must-have-at-all-costs equations that generate stress, anxiety, and less than ideal creative situations, binding us to specific results, thereby drowning our highest potential in a sea of tension.

The call now is to harness our power and become increasingly comfortable in our own skin as we begin to see ourselves in a new light—powerful, eternal, intuitive, creative blended beings who flow *with* life rather than force life through rigid, outdated expectations and hidden agendas that demand life show up in only one way.

Knowing the difference between forcing something and flow is especially important when it comes to raising children. When we navigate life from soul, we make our *own* daily assessment of where to invest our energy. We discern where we desire to focus, and look carefully at the ways in which our thoughts, words, and actions quite naturally reflect where our energy goes. A mucky focus of energy will tend to create a mucky result. In any situation or relationship, it serves us to pause every so often to assess our focus so that we become clear about the energy we offer to the world at large.

It behooves us to recognize as early as possible our infinite capacity to choose and create from a heartfelt place of self-love, oneness, tolerance, and compassion for all. If we are parents, we must lay the groundwork by first integrating these truths for ourselves, then modeling for our children what it means to be a conscious global citizen. Modeling for our children the subtle yet highly beneficial balance of inner focus—contemplation, observation, reflection, receptivity, and awe—with the outer focus of proactivity and productivity is vital. If we can teach our children to utilize this continual intake and outtake of their own energy, they will become the powerful conscious creators they are meant to be.

Children need to know they are an integral part of the oneness, and that conscious focus flows from awareness of oneness with everyone and everything. Through your example, show them how to recognize patterns of inattention that may be moving positive energy away from a desired purpose. One of the best ways to do this is to allow natural consequences to arise. When these aren't to a child's liking, help the child make changes in their energy output to keep them on course. It may be helpful to assist a child with making a list of the different thoughts, words, and actions that lead to what they are experiencing in their lives, showing them how to categorize these energetic offerings as either expansive or detrimental to their intended purpose. Share your own heart's desires and the energetic pathways you utilize to fulfill them.

As our children exercise their gifts as conscious creators, focusing their energy where they truly desire, they will discover their ability to capture the rapture and experience their own divinity through their lives lived.

SHIFT

#9

From Self-Betrayal to Self-Love

From People Pleasing to Boundaries
From Self-Sabotage to Freedom
From False Humility to True Power
From Subconscious Code to Soul Code
From Diplomacy to Truth
From Indirect to Forthright

I am not afraid of my truth anymore, and I will not omit pieces of me to make you comfortable.
Author Unknown

Creating boundaries through self-love paradoxically deepens our experience of everyday oneness. For it's only when we can be true to ourselves that we feel comfortable getting up-close-and-personal with others.

We live in a culture in which few love themselves, and it's this lack of self-love that produces the narcissism that's a hallmark of our time. When I speak of a lack of self-love, I'm referring to the people-pleasing epidemic. Our world would change overnight from the largely hostile place it is to a planet that welcomes everyone, were we all to worry less about pleasing the other. No one benefits when we are tightly ensconced in the status quo at the expense of who we truly are.

We each need to live true in every dimension of our lives, courageously and passionately embracing our quirkiness, oddness, unique vantage points, and all. It's the small self-betrayals day in and day out that build and build until they wreak havoc. The price of self-betrayal in the name of empathy, compassion, generosity, selflessness, and diplomacy becomes too high. Why is it that we offer these highly regarded attributes to everyone but ourselves?

When the reality of my self-betrayal awakened me in the middle of the night, rising up from an anguished place deep inside, I was aghast and saddened. Throughout my entire life, I had daily said yes to others at the expense of my own soul. As I wept, I understood that self-betrayal is the lowest kind of betrayal. This realization became the key to ensuring that from here on out, I would only say yes to others if it didn't mean having to say no to my soul. The relief that this realization brought me has never left me. Every choice is now filtered through soul.

Reshaping our life from role to soul means disentangling from what no longer serves our truth, and therefore no longer really serves the truth of another. While at first we're likely to feel uncomfortable as we get used to a new lens, it's one of the most liberating steps I've ever taken in my personal development. Unless we are "selfish" enough to love ourselves by living true, we have nothing to offer other than a mere shell. This is because, behind any perceived gift, the real gift is the energy of love and integrity that supports it. Both must be in alignment to offer something that truly uplifts.

So many of my thoughts, words, and actions were based on what I thought others needed from me, which was largely a matter of me being seen as a "good" girl. There's no freedom in this, only endless half-truths, resentment, and ultimately anger. Nearing the end of this life pattern, I at times felt a subtle strain on my heart when I betrayed my soul in the name of not betraying another. It was the strain of a lifetime of apologizing for my own light, forsaking myself, allowing others to pull me into their sphere of influence. I began to feel "unsafe" around certain individuals with whom this pattern of engagement was particularly embedded. My heart beat faster, sweat poured from my underarms, and my insides churned. My body registered the price of self-betrayal, as sometimes it took up to an hour to settle after an interaction.

What Humility Really Is

As a child I was taught by my well-meaning mother to be "humble." In our family that meant hiding your light under a bushel—something Jesus said not to do. This gross misunderstanding of humility denied me my power as a person.

It wasn't all bad, since empathy, observation, and deep listening flourished—qualities that have served me well. However, these qualities shouldn't be at the expense of our personal power, but should function as an adjunct to our assertiveness, strength, and resilience.

I was taught to play small so as never to outshine another, to hold back, to never make something about me, to be self-deprecating, and to fly under the radar so as not to be seen or heard too frequently or loudly. And, of course, I was to be diplomatic at all costs, not realizing that a mask of diplomacy not only chips away at our integrity but wreaks havoc with our well-being mentally, emotionally, and ultimately physically.

A caveat: When I speak of diplomacy, I don't mean *how* a message is delivered, but rather the truth of the message. I always seek to offer my words or actions with kindness and warmth whenever possible.

As an example of what "humble" meant in my mom's

eyes back then, my unwillingness to make anything about me led to asking friends lots of questions so that their answers filled the space—a way of avoiding claiming my own space and self-disclosing. This stemmed from the belief I wasn't important enough to be part of any significant equation. Ego-inversion rather than ego-inflation was the name of the game—itself a form of ego since it too is part of the false self. In short, I was to apologize for being me!

Consequently, when a good friend held a joint book publishing party for myself and another friend in our town who had also recently published a book, I didn't embrace it as a well-deserved celebration of my accomplishment. Instead I made it more about the other author. As I held my book in my hands the following day, I felt furious with myself, realizing I hadn't only betrayed myself but also my book. I had poured my heart and soul into this book, then totally downplayed it, treating it almost with embarrassment—as if my friend's lighter, humorous book was more of a mainstream fit.

On another occasion, as my husband and I were waiting to congratulate our own son on a great baseball game and take him out to lunch, a man came up to us and began going on and on to my husband, a teacher and a coach, about his own kid. We stood there for about thirty minutes listening and nodding. Afterwards both my husband and I felt angry with ourselves for allowing someone to monopolize our time at an inappropriate moment that considered only his agenda. This wasn't about listening, which is a positive trait, but about being railroaded.

My breakthrough came during the time of severe physical duress I wrote about earlier, when I endured a nine-month ordeal with my lower back. The evening of this breakthrough, my husband and I were out. We ran into another couple, which led to a conversation that caused me to feel stress on my heart as a result of passive bullying on the part of the woman, who was strong-arming me into disclosing aspects of myself I didn't wish to share. When the conversation ended, I realized I had betrayed myself. It was at 4 a.m. that I awakened with alarming pain running down my left leg, as if the nerve was on fire. The pain was so excruciating that it all but compelled me to finally navigate the passage from self-betrayal to self-love. Before waking, I had been dreaming about a glowing cord pulsating with love from head to toe on that side of my body.

To find my voice felt like an enormous weight had been lifted off me. Once I acclimated to the pronounced shift in perspective, with the feeling of relief came anger at myself for playing nice to appease others. Eventually I forgave myself, as I increasingly not only accepted but proactively loved the "Annie" I now found myself to be. What a relief to be free of fear that others might disappoint me, hurt me, not include me, dislike me, not accept me, tease me, find fault with me, chastise me, punish me, or burn me for simply being me. As I mentioned, my mother had instilled in me that flying under the radar was the way to be safe. The truth is, it's our power—our own light—that's scary, which is why we imagine that to live safely we must hide it.

With my particular glass ceiling shattered, my mom's kind of humble was no longer for me. I was learning now how to come from strength in every situation, and what a difference it made. For instance, I had been taught it was selfish to be inflexible and that I ought to compromise by giving in to the wishes of others. Not realizing I was compromising *myself* much of the time, I allowed my mask to become a persona of flexibility. "It doesn't matter to me; you decide," was my common response. I didn't understand that compromise is settling for the lowest common denominator, which makes no one truly happy.

As someone once said, if you want potatoes and I want beef, but I don't really like potatoes and you don't really like beef, making hash just makes a hash of everything.

A far better way of handling conflicting desires is to brainstorm from a place of owning our power, which has a way of producing unexpected win-win solutions. It also teaches us that we aren't Siamese twins emotionally, with two heads both trying to control a single body. Emotional maturity involves developing the ability to occupy our *own* space. Going with the flow from awareness of our power honors our individuality within the oneness, so that neither cancels out the other. Solving issues from strength and resilience has a completely different feel and effect than capitulating to someone else's wishes.

Since my eyes were opened to my self-betrayal, my mom and I have talked and cried together, coming to terms with the things I've shared here. While she admitted that my truth sometimes scared her, she unhesitatingly and lovingly gave me permission to soar. Such unconditional love, offered whether I was a "good" girl or not, felt divine.

Humility isn't about playing small. Humility is a realistic appraisal of ourselves. Said differently, it's functioning from an awakened state—full throttle.

A Recent Project, Giving Away My Power, and a Sore Tailbone

When a shift happens, we don't usually get the whole package in a single go. The lesson has to be reinforced, sometimes painfully. This was the case with beginning to trust my own judgment in my work.

Over the course of several months, I worked with another individual on a project that ultimately never landed fully in physical reality. While it could be looked upon as a failure—lost time, energy, and money—for me it proved to be yet another priceless cycle of learning, inviting me to trust myself implicitly.

In working with a partner on back end details to grow *my* work—one with whom I was creating a business venture and splitting profits 50-50—I found myself succumbing to her insistence upon *one* right way to succeed. I felt she knew better when it came to business, since she had been trained by the "big boys" and had years of experience. I saw her as mentoring me on the high-yielding ways of content marketing.

I confess I was a little scared to take this project on and looked to this woman to push me into the big league in my field. I felt that perhaps my work wasn't enough while simply growing in the way that felt good to me. Following this initial resistance, I came to believe that it was *I* who was afraid of growing my work bigger. It was I who was afraid to self-promote and close the deal. It was I who needed to follow another's lead on all matters even when it was *my* life's work that was on the line.

Being stretched in new ways can be invigorating. But stretching for stretching's sake means nothing if we lose our grounding in the process. As the weeks wore on, and the project became more and more complex—with all the hours billed on my dime—I became increasingly uncomfortable and ungrounded. Losing connection to my own core, my tailbone started to ache. Standing, sitting, lying down, there was an ache in my lower chakra.

I have an unyielding vision for my work, and that vision is transparency, integrity, freedom, and truth for *all* involved. This vision matches *exactly* the vision for my life. A project, a business endeavor, a friendship, a marriage, an extracurricular activity—none of these work for me unless they resonate with my soul. I desire my offerings to be mutually beneficial. This is what works *for me*.

You'll have realized by now that I'm not someone who

could sell sugary products to poverty-stricken areas in the name of increasing profits. I couldn't open a string of liquor stores in depressed areas to line my own pockets. I would never own a company in which the top dog takes millions while the lowest rung employees make minimum wage. Consequently, when it became apparent that there was a somewhat gimmicky vibe to this woman's approach to marketing my work, it didn't sit well with me.

No doubt the approach I was exposed to is working well for others in similar fields—for some even to the tune of millions. I, however, felt disempowered by the whole experience, and my sweet little tailbone wasn't going to let me off the hook until I regained *my* center, focus, creativity, and sense of self.

Though money was lost, I was drawn to this experience; as is often the case, it was not for what could be gained monetarily but for what could be learned through an experience of opposites. In the final days of the project, I realized I didn't really want it to succeed. The energy felt disharmonious.

Although I realized I had again been tempted to trust someone other than my own soul, I wasn't discouraged. On the contrary, my connection with soul was increasingly coming alive. For example, I noticed I was excited to create pages of notes on how I would try again in my own way next time. The sparkle in my eyes reappeared as I imagined meshing a few of the new ideas with my own voice, leaving aside anything that didn't resonate.

I would rather continue to grow both personally and professionally in the organic way that works for me than push my way to the top and lose my greatest asset—my connection to the voice of my own soul. This was a painful lesson, yet I felt free to be me again. Oh, and my tailbone was thrilled!

Family and Friends May Not Like What You Do—So What?

Some of my family members and friends are, to say the least, not interested in what I do. Some even view it as useless psycho-spiritual babble. More than a few don't read my blogs, which I consider to be straight from my soul.

I no longer feel wounded, though perhaps sometimes pricked, when I get wind of someone I'm relatively close to who doesn't appreciate my work and perhaps even belittles it. I've had to realize that not everyone is going to believe in what I do or even see who I really am. Just because an individual is our spouse, child, parent, sister, brother, or close college friend doesn't mean we will grow in the same direction.

From my perspective, our most precious gift to one another is to encourage personal development, but this isn't a reality in many relationships. Another's growth can even be felt as a threat. However, a lack of validation from others is no reason to hold back. To be truly free, we must break away from old family patterns and dynamics and move into our most authentic self. The ability to *self-validate* is the key to moving forward.

Self-validation means we don't need others to believe in what we do. They may even feel we're full of shit. Apart from the slight prick I experience at the time, I've become okay with this. I can't expect someone to be supportive just because they love me, even though I may be supportive of them. I've learned not to expect reciprocation.

Relationships can be powerful pathways to personal development. Seen in this light, if we get pricked, some area of our lives is being reflected back to us in which we aren't yet whole—aren't yet self-validated.

Don't expect your loved ones and close friends always to get what you do, or even to respect it. They don't need to.

SHIFT
#10

From Extreme Empathy to True Service

FROM MERGING WITH ANOTHER'S DARKNESS TO SIMPLY SHINING LIGHT
FROM HALF LOVE TO HIGHER LOVE
FROM ENABLING TO HELPING
FROM SAVING ANOTHER TO INVITING ANOTHER
FROM DOING TO MODELING

My barn having burned to the ground, I can now see the moon.
TAOIST SAYING

Have you ever felt angry with individuals who are unwilling to self-examine, and who instead live on the surface of their own life and project their psychic debris onto others? I have, and I came to see that much of my anger is actually directed toward *myself* for allowing myself to feel it was my duty to carry another's sludge. I felt I shouldn't make them feel bad for their unwillingness to do their own inner work.

I figured that to create an environment in which others could feel good about themselves, no matter what their output, was simply my cross to bear, as if the onus for others' good behavior and personal development somehow fell on me.

Always empathic, I was actually attracted to another's darkness, thinking that I both *could* and *needed* to save them. Empathy as a way of perceiving the world was my main lens for almost as long as I can remember. While a healthy level of empathy is a hallmark of a blended being, I developed a pattern detrimental to not only myself but also others, as a result of extreme empathy—identifying first with the other person's feelings rather than my own. I learned many lessons due to this, one of which nearly cost me my life.

Extreme empathy is quite tricky because we feel we are being of service to others, and don't realize we're betraying not only ourselves but also the individual we believe we're assisting. To be of service to another, there's never a need to take on or filter through ourselves another's darkness, which is precisely what we do in extreme empathy. Real service to another is always grounded in awareness. Hence we must deepen our understanding of both the light and the dark if we are to be of service. If we identify darkness and are unable to stay within our own sphere of light, it's better to walk away and not engage. We don't go where we are uninvited. Instead, we allow our light to radiate. Great leaders such as Martin Luther King, Gandhi, and Jesus understood this distinction, and for this reason their service was of a higher quality than most.

I had to learn that another person's darkness isn't mine to process, as the price would always be too high for all involved. The point is for others to meet us in the light, not us meet them in the darkness. To merge with another's darkness rather than invite them to recognize their own light is a disservice to all. We offer light not so that we can become an escape from their darkness, but as a mirror of the light in their own center. A brilliantly lit example on the outside is much more powerful than walking with them as a small flashlight in their own dark tunnel. Carrying or processing another's psychic debris only intensifies their darkness—their unconsciousness. Not only do I not have to go into their darkness to be a bridge for them, but today if the other doesn't wish to cross the bridge into their own wholeness, I simply bless them and move on.

Turning off extreme empathy and instead focusing on extending my positivity to others through my own wholeness, expanded heart, and authenticity is proving to be much more uplifting to people than drowning in their darkness right along with them. I now know that others are more than capable of developing in their own way. I can be a guiding light if a mutually felt opportunity arises, but it's not my job to save another, and in fact it's misguided and even arrogant to believe that being a vehicle of service for the oneness would presume another's path needs to unfold according to my insights and standards.

The way I offer my light is by simply being myself. Through my awareness of soul, I inspire others to embrace their own soul. By living out my personal expression of the oneness, I offer people a clear choice between their light and their darkness. It then becomes their decision to process their darkness so that they can move into their own light. I have nothing to do with their actual choice other than showing up as an example of what's possible.

The Trap of Extreme Empathy

Since butterfly season is upon us as I write, it feels appropriate to share the story of the boy and the butterfly. While I'm unsure where this story originated, a member of my Soul to Soul Circle reminds us of it often, always helping us remember our place when it comes to holding space for another's challenges.

A little boy finds a caterpillar and takes it home to observe the cocooning process. Oh, how the boy loves his new friend, visiting immediately upon waking, after school, and before bed. It seems like eons to the boy, but finally the caterpillar cocoons, and the boy at first remains patiently watchful of the transformation taking place. But soon, with the best of intentions, he decides to help break open the cocoon to assist the butterfly, which after a short time dies in his hands.

A butterfly's wings grow stronger with each day that it has to push against the walls of its cocoon to break free. So also a soul evolves by journeying through each facet of the multilayered process of self-development. Whether we deem what's happening to them good or bad, allowing others to experience the ups and downs of their lives is vital for each soul's development. The minute we feel ourselves becoming hooked into another's particular challenge and take it on as our own, it's time to step back.

One of my favorite picture books for adults, as well as children, is entitled *Hope for the Flowers* by Trina Paulus. "How does one become a butterfly?" she asks. The answer is, "You must want to fly so much that you are willing to give up being a caterpillar." Extreme empathy is a deterrent to a caterpillar's desire to fly!

Often the energy behind the helpful thoughts, words, and actions we extend towards others in the name of compassion is laced with pity. Along with the helping hand, the donor subconsciously doles out an energetic belief that matches the "unfortunate" situation, actually helping to sustain the energy surrounding the person's sad state of affairs.

Compassion isn't an *I can do it for you* vibe, but a *you can do it for yourself* vibe. In other words, the most beneficial offering we can ever give someone is to *see and feel* them as they *really* are beyond their physical masks and current predicament. It's their highest potential as a self-realized soul that we hope to ignite through our contribution, which is quite different from reinforcing their perceived stuck condition or misfortune.

Compassion that leads to healing comes through nothing less than a heightened awareness of the other's divine essence. Acknowledgement of this as we offer the warm cup of coffee, the used clothing, or the financial donation is of utmost importance to both giver and receiver, since it's the energy exchange that really seals the deal.

The trick is to give a gift that keeps on giving, which we can do by offering compassion without pity to those in need. When we do so, we give them an infusion of empowering energy that speaks volumes without a word being said. This only happens to the degree we really see the individual before us, feeling their presence, acknowledging their magnificence as an aspect of infinite divine essence.

Moving Beyond Self-denying Empathy

My pattern of extreme empathy was closely tied to my mother complex, which as I discussed in the previous chapter invited self-betrayal. I learned it was my job to save the world—a strange paradox, given that I was also to play small and fly under the radar. I learned it was my duty to see the world through the eyes of others and offer service by merging into their darkness energetically. In other words, the weight of the darkness throughout the world was on my shoulders even without the honor of owning my own light.

This was a heavy burden. No wonder that, at age thirteen, the first sign of back problems appeared, causing me to give up my beloved ballet, which I had enjoyed immensely since the age of four. Dancing was a natural gateway for me, so this sacrifice was symbolic of the high cost of extreme empathy. Little wonder that is was during my back issue, which resulted in neurosurgery, that my need to show extreme empathy lifted once and for all.

Today I find that if I encounter a situation in which extreme empathy would have previously been my response and I begin to allow myself to buy into it, within twelve hours my body will let me know. I can feel in my back and heart any tendency to move in that direction.

When this happens, I simply breathe and realign myself with my own light. I don't beat myself up, and I don't avoid new situations in the name of protecting myself. But even if someone is mid-sentence, and I feel the old pattern within me, I gently disengage until I'm ready to interact from a place of empathy rather than extreme empathy. From this re-centering, I acknowledge to myself that I don't have to solve anything for the other, as it disempowers both them and me.

I now love myself too much to carelessly and unconsciously block my own light in the name of assisting another with their darkness. While it may seem less than compassionate to some, it's just the opposite. Compassion—right alongside true service—abounds in this shift. There's no limit to what can be offered through this more self-preserving and neutral lens. We can help many more people if we avoid extreme empathy.

Soul is about truth, and extreme empathy hides truth. My niceness, diplomacy, and general discomfort with another's discomfort served only to keep them in darkness. In the name of helping them and loving them, I was blocking their self-development. Who am I to peel back the walls of their cocoon before they have had the chance to sufficiently develop their wings against its walls? We can help hold the space for another's growth through listening, since silence is often more powerful than talking. We can even share insights when asked. But we never enter the space as our own.

When working with others, I recognize I can integrate unintegrated aspects of myself while simultaneously being of the highest service. In this way my example becomes a teaching tool. Only when this really clicks for us can true service begin, not before.

To fan the flames for another from our own life lived is our sole contribution. This honors the fact that everyone is an inherently powerful being in their own right—no matter what their journey, their misfortune. In the oneness, all is well just as it is. Consequently there's no one to save. How could there be, when there's only a single brilliant light?

I sobbed as I finally realized that when I carried the load of so many others, thinking of myself as a good, kind person, I was unknowingly being unkind to both myself and them. I could hardly believe how misguided my lens of extreme empathy had been, and I felt much grief over the wasted energy.

I'm encouraged by the myth of Psyche and Aphrodite. In order to assist Psyche in becoming a whole woman who could make space for *all* aspects of the divine feminine—such as intuition, creativity, and empowerment, not just empathy—Aphrodite assigned her four tasks. The final task involved crossing a blood river whereby she must save herself rather than allow herself to drown with all the others in the river who were reaching for help from those who were already drowning. In trying to save them to no avail, she too would have drowned, leaving no survivors. It was a heart-wrenching choice, but in the end she chose to save herself.

Moment by moment, day by day, and soul to soul, we must use our inner guidance system to know when, where, and how to be of service as a *space holder* for another, but not a container for them. We must *feel* service rather than think it, always remembering that self-loving boundaries are where meaningful service begins.

Anti-Bullying or Pro-Acceptance?

We are constantly exchanging energy with one another, and the quality of these exchanges matters so much more than most realize. If we want to serve in a way that brings real change to the world, the first step is to clean up our own energy field, which means becoming aware that if things aren't going well in our life, it's not just the coach's fault, the teacher's fault, the bank's fault, or the supervisor's fault. Instead of passing the buck, we examine our role in any interaction, then make those choices that reflect who we really are. In other words, if we are to make a difference in the world, it matters *how* we focus on change. Our approach can't be hostile—can't be one of attacking the dark. It needs to be one of shedding our light. Hence the priority needs to be self-transformation first, activism second.

Bullying is a hot topic currently. It's a form of hostility that's rife all over the planet; it manifests in the ways that governments dictate to their people, managers ride roughshod over the needs of workers, teachers lord it over pupils, students bully one another on the playground, parents dominate their children, and children and adults of both genders are abused sexually.

After watching the movie *Bully* with my children, I cried because the superficial way we try to solve this issue is so inadequate. Bullying is seen as a "battle" we're fighting. While being anti-bullying and pro-acceptance appear to be the same, they carry a distinctly different vibe. If we want to create change in our world, it's important to recognize this. Anti-bullying, the war on drugs, the fight against poverty, and the war on cancer all push *against* something. This is fundamentally different from being pro-acceptance, helping people become free from addiction, promoting abundance for all, and celebrating and fostering wellness.

When we push really hard against something, we are actually focusing a powerful stream of energy towards it. In the aforementioned examples, that stream of energy pours into what we *do not want*, so that instead of eliminating it, we bolster it. As the saying is, "The energy flows where the attention goes."

Where has the war on drugs gotten us? The war on cancer? The fight against crime? The war on terrorism? Isn't it becoming obvious that a "war" on something or a "fight" against something never solves the problem? Declaring war on something often simply sends it underground, rendering it even more difficult to overcome. In the process, such a warring mentality creates separatist, exclusivist vibes, which ultimately disconnect individuals and groups from their original intent.

Does a movement elevate the human spirit? Does it bring hope? Does it empower? How about fostering freedom, appreciation, joy, and truth? As we've been seeing, initiating change involves shedding light, not plunging into the darkness. Notice the different *feeling* in your body and in your heart that results from a "war on cancer" versus a celebration of wellness. Or to take a different example, which feels best to you: being anti-big government or pro-individual responsibility?

If the vibe pouring into a movement is one of me against you—a vibe of condemnation, hatred, resentment, or anger—expect an outcome of *more of the same*. The effectiveness of any movement will mirror the energy we put into it.

Compassion Unplugged

As I've increasingly cleaned up my energy field, I've found myself getting back in touch with a place deep inside; that first came to my attention when I was a young girl growing up in Norfolk, Virginia, where I was exposed to racial and economic diversity on a daily basis through both my local public school and a mother who discussed openly the invisible divisions and subsequent disparities.

I can remember as clear as a bell being in my first grade classroom and, as I observed others around me, intuiting what it meant to be underprivileged in a world that values privilege. I could sense other people's suffering quite acutely within myself. While I remember doing well in school academically, those early years were much more about deepening an empathic well that, for me, became the most natural way to view the world.

Later in life, it was a surprise to discover that extreme empathy—viewing and feeling the world first and foremost in the way others felt it—not only wasn't how everyone else perceived the world, but that it was an imbalance in myself that needed correcting. Imagine my surprise when I discovered that forsaking the yearnings of my own soul in the name of empathy, generosity, kindness, and compassion wasn't really virtuous after all.

This turned out to be only one side of the coin. For I learned that while my self-love was growing, I didn't yet have the capacity for the truest and highest kind of service. As I developed boundaries, surprisingly my compassion didn't wane but was enhanced—to the point I've felt the wide humanitarian lens of my past returning, though in a new light. At last bathed in self-worth, I am finally ready to serve meaningfully.

As I noticed myself yearning to serve in new ways, I began clipping ideas from my beloved Chicago Tribune, since it too was exploring ways we can uplift the underprivileged. As my passion began to flow in a new direction, it felt strangely familiar—that of the compassionate young girl whose soul is today the heartbeat of my being. As I explained earlier, a child's natural leanings are often clues to their gateways in adult life.

An intense love for humanity seems uncontainable

to me some days. I call those kinds of days "big love" days, where the love is directed towards *all* rather than remaining primarily a personal love for "mine." Around this time, my beautiful daughters began answering a call to participate in service-exploration trips that will take them around the globe in the years to come. As their perspective widens, so does mine, leading to a collaborative sharing of our similar hopes for the future in discussions that evidence a palpable excitement at the possibilities. In fact, my girls will be up and running and able to offer their unique gifts to the world much sooner than I, since there's less psychic debris to wade through when you've not only been truly seen and heard by your parents, but allowed to be fully and safely yourself within the nest.

SHIFT
#11

From Diminishment to Mutuality

FROM COMPETITION TO SPACE FOR ALL
FROM INTIMIDATION TO OWNERSHIP
FROM EXPERT TO EQUAL
FROM TEACHER/STUDENT TO TWO SOULS
FROM HIDDEN AGENDA TO TRANSPARENCY
FROM COMPARISON TO SELF-ACCEPTANCE
FROM SHOULD TO EITHER PARTAKE OR PASS
FROM GIVING AWAY POWER TO EMPOWERMENT

You shall no longer take things at second or third hand. Nor look through the eyes of the dead, nor feed on the specters in books. You shall not look through my eyes either, nor take things from me. You shall listen to all sides and filter them from yourself.
WALT WHITMAN

We've all felt it at one time or another. A friend shares a success story or a great idea for what's sure to be a future success story, and we gush with praise and excitement on the outside. But on the *inside*, not so much. Or that photo on Facebook in which our friend shines with style and beauty at a high-powered function to a crowd of adoring "likes," whereas we work from home and haven't gotten out of our workout clothes or gone out much beyond the supermarket or carpool in days. And how about when a good friend has found a way to create a business that not only makes money, but also involves their lifelong passion—and it matches what we'd love to create?

Several years ago, I looked at this shadow aspect of myself. I wrestled with wanting the best for my friends, while simultaneously being afraid their success somehow diminished me. I remember as far back as ballet class, when as a child of seven I danced six days a week with strict teachers from Romania. They were hard on students in a way we would deem unacceptable today. I recall a mixture of sadness and joy when the teachers picked on my friends instead of me. I equally remember feeling a mixture of sadness and joy when my teachers praised my friends instead of me.

Don't all of us experience shame for kind of wanting the best for our friends, and kind of not?

It's taken me years to really get that another's success has nothing to do with me except that it expands the energetic possibility for *all* of us to succeed with our own dreams. Not only are we not diminished, but the opportunities don't shrink because another is out there shining their light. The universe is infinite and responds to our vibes in a way science is just beginning to uncover. We are all mini creators in our own unique space. Another can't ever actually create in *our* space, regardless of our misperception that they can.

Not always capable of being fully happy for friends in their moments of triumph, I often found it easier to support them when they were low. As I shone light on this aspect of myself, not only acknowledging it but also accepting it, I realized it was left over from a childhood fear that there wouldn't be enough of everything to go around.

When I learn of another's success and can't be wholly happy for them, I recognize it as the sting of self-doubt about my own capabilities. Self-doubt has been at the core of almost all my life themes—the feeling that I'm *not good enough*. With me it tends to take the form of trusting others more than I trust myself. Hence shedding self-doubt has been among the more rewarding shifts for me, since the results can be readily felt with every choice I make. When we choose empowerment over giving away our power, the effect can be felt throughout the body. Likewise, when we choose diminishment, the agony reminds us we haven't yet fully integrated this shift. Both act as a barometer.

A Different Perspective on Teacher and Student

Comparing ourselves with others, so that we either feel superior or inferior, is such a waste of energy—an insight that was hammered home for me when I was invited to be a presenter for a breakout session at The Festival of Enlightenment in Colorado. From my Soul to Soul Circles and public talks, I had already begun to realize that teacher and student share the same space—that teaching and learning are two sides of the same coin. But I really got the point when, at this event in Colorado, I arrived at the room I was supposed to speak in and found it locked because no one had signed up. I looked at the schedule and attended a fellow speaker's talk instead. As I listened to this speaker, I realized the seats of teacher and student are interchangeable and felt buoyed with joy.

No matter what anyone else offers, it doesn't diminish our authentic offering. There's space for all. The only way our contribution can be diminished is if we push negatively against another's, thereby distancing ourselves from our own soul, since our soul is ultimately one with the person we're pushing against.

As a blended being, we understand there's no competition for our soul purpose. We are the *only* ones who can be *us* and do what we do. Realizing this, we stop focusing on what we feel may be lacking in what we have to offer—what we *aren't*—and focus on what we *are* as fully operational beings with our own unique gifts. Whatever we do, it needs to flow from our truth, so that we offer it with love and in a way that always honors the other. In this way, what we produce becomes sacred, not an unconscious crapshoot. In this way we function as an individuated vehicle for the oneness.

Since I teach what I need to integrate more fully, my workshops are as beneficial to me as to those who take part. In other words, I unstick myself as I help others to become unstuck, so that we are souls exchanging what's required for transformation. This is very much the case with this book. I don't pretend to be a religious scholar, spiritual leader, enlightened master, or any other label that most people feel might give me the authority to discuss such topics. I'm simply me, a blended being on this beautiful planet evolving into her own truth like everyone else. To me, sharing from this perspective is the new model—less about experts and much more about ordinary individuals each sharing from their extraordinary vantage point. We have much to learn from one another's daily contemplations and discoveries, which only increases as we each move into a deeper intimacy with our unique expression of soul in physical form. A wise teacher and an eager student live deep inside us all, and their collaboration creates the optimal atmosphere for personal development.

Realizing this, if constructive criticism is offered by another, we learn to discern whether it's truly about us or about *them*. All of us are on our own journey of awakening, replete with past conditioning, which means we can never be a pure guide for someone else. While we may certainly ask for assistance and insight on any and all topics, the voice of our own soul is the final arbiter of what's true for us.

Since the guru is always us, it's necessary we own this. In my teaching, I used to put the emphasis on others. Now I realize that if my name is on it, then it needs to reflect me—my authenticity, my voice, my energy. In my eyes these days there are no "experts," simply other blended beings with different passions, experiences, bases of knowledge, and vantage points.

No One Can Diminish Us But Ourselves

With this shift comes a move from hidden agendas to transparency, as we realize there's no other way for a blended being to live true. Soul-to-soul exchanges don't foster untruths, denials, underbellies, and backhandedness. If a situation or institution doesn't allow for transparency, we have the option to pass.

Several do similar work as me in my local area. In one case our practices are less than a mile apart. We share many participants who overlap in my Soul to Soul Circles and in her classes. Though I always had a high regard for her work, initially I felt some competition with her. As I became more confident in offering what I truly enjoy, I realized that this wonderful teacher being so close by—like two restaurants on the same block—helped create the fertile ground for awakening in our community for which my soul longs. The vortex of energy is stronger as a result of both of us sharing space. With the competitive spirit released, the energy then changed, which manifested in the fruits.

Another friend and I do similar work, even blogging in the same venues. When a wonderful blog of hers went viral, I was happy for her—though it also brought up for me the old feeling of not being good enough. Due to our friendship, we discuss feelings as they arise, and she and I experience the empowerment derived from watching someone we love develop and offer their gifts to the world.

After my first book *Soul to Soul Parenting* had been published, I came in from a walk to discover online that a new book of a similar premise and title had hit bookstores. My stomach knotted as I frantically examined this wonderful book. While I wrestled with anxiety over which book might sell better, at the same time I realized my soul didn't care about sales. Several months later this book won the gold Nautilus award and mine the silver in the parenting category. I had to laugh because by this time I had reached out to the author, and we had become colleagues and friends. I hosted her on my radio show and we have endorsed each other's work. Her book has gone on to sell more copies than mine. Her following on social media is larger than mine. Yet I engage in neither comparison nor competition with this beautiful blended being. Her work is divine, and so is mine.

Learning to Believe in My Calling

A variety of incidents began to dispel my self-doubt where my work was concerned. I learned that people have their own agendas, which don't necessarily equate with my best interests. Through these, my belief in the uniqueness of my calling and trust in my ability to carry it out gradually became rock solid.

In the first incident, following my appearance on a radio show, the host went into a diatribe on all the ways I could have improved my answers. With no broadcasting experience under my belt, I found myself feeling increasingly uncomfortable. Was the reason for this that my work was indeed inadequate? Or was my discomfort arising from feeling imprisoned by this individual's "lecture"? When he offered me the chance to participate in one of his expensive workshops to better my media expertise, it was confirmation of my sense that his criticism, touted as "constructive," had a thinly veiled agenda that had little to do with my interviewing skills.

I had a similar experience with an expert who reviewed my book after its publication and proceeded to rip it apart, sharing that if he had been given the chance to edit it for me, the project would have been turned upside down and inside out to its benefit. While there were other reviews that sometimes weren't stellar—among many that were—after only a few hours of twirling about this individual's opinion of my work, I chose not to give my power away by succumbing to the criticism. In this case, what was said didn't feel like a match for what I knew to be true about my imperfect yet authentic first book.

After being asked to be one of eight speakers to each deliver a twelve-minute talk about our work to a group of community leaders such as PTA presidents, with a view to utilizing us for more extensive presentations at their places of work, I quickly understood that mine stood out as the different one, since the others were secular and mine more spiritual. The gist of the comments afterwards was that my talk was moving but too spiritual for school-related audiences. By now I was far enough into this shift to accept the comments with a content soul, while also realizing I was unwilling to water down my offering. With this, I knew that my empowerment was here to stay.

It's for this reason that, in this book, I chose to use the terms "oneness" for what many refer to as God or Spirit, and "soul" for individuated aspects of the oneness. Many use "soul" and "spirit" (no capital s on the word spirit) to mean the individual divine flame that manifests as this particular body, and Spirit (with a capital S) to refer to the oneness or God. I have opted to use soul and oneness instead of spirit and Spirit to express the larger perspective and smaller perspective in a uniform manner that's true to my own journey. As what people refer to as "the spiritual path" was my path for a long time, it's language that has always felt like home to me. I write with the understanding that an individuated soul is one aspect of a much larger eternal flame that's multifaceted, multidimensional, non-physical, and much, much more than what we are talking about here as part of this particular incarnation.

You may be surprised I don't use a capital O on the word oneness. This book is about what it means to live free of dualism. This involves a recognition that not only is soul not some ethereal component housed in a body, as discussed in Part I, but that the whole of existence is an expression of the oneness. As I'll address more fully in the next chapter, there's *no separation* between sacred and secular, holy and profane. Such categories are the product of unawakened minds and simply don't exist for the awakened person.

When we put a capital g on the word God, it inevitably implies something separate from the creation, as a capital O on the word oneness also tends to do. When I read the writings of spiritual teachers, more and more I see the use of capital letters on all kinds of words, each use intended to denote a "higher" state—Higher Self, Higher Purpose, Love, Abundance, Intention, Wholeness, Healing, and on and on. Almost any word seems subject to capitalization today. In fact, I used to be the queen of this. What I used to be unaware of is that *this fosters a subtle dualism—separation thinking*. The capitalized entity is portrayed as somehow "other," which is just another manifestation of what's been a major blindness of religion and many spiritualists from time immemorial.

The point I make in this book is that *there is no higher state, no "other" reality*. We are living—and living in—the divine!

Dualism has a way of creeping in so surreptitiously—an illustration of how resistant we are to fully owning the divinity of our natural being and the creation all around us.

I'm no longer hesitant, let alone afraid, to claim—and bask in!—my divine heritage—and I don't need to write "Divine Heritage" to do so.

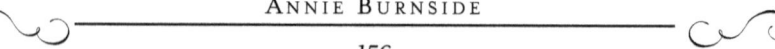

My Project Is Not Gonna Be Good Enough

I was honored to be a speaker at an education symposium at Marian University in Indiana and excitedly drove to Indianapolis for the event. Upon arrival, and knowing only the host of the event, I took my seat and awaited the introductions and the two keynotes of the evening.

The Power Points, rich with research and data, not to mention the speakers' degrees and the number of books they had written, triggered the frightening thought, "I'm at the wrong conference. Do the planners *really* know what I do? Is it too late to back out?"

It was a pattern that dated back to when I was ten, and I quickly recognized it for what it was. When I brought to school a project I'd worked on tirelessly and saw everyone else's projects, I became alarmed, thinking, "My project isn't good enough." Which of course led to me telling myself, "*I'm* not good enough."

As I sat in the audience in the row of other presenters, rather than resist my feelings, I embraced them, soothing myself. I thought back to what I was like at ten, imagined myself hugging myself, and was soon holding hands with myself, smiling as I careened down a long slide. A flash of insight for the introduction to my talk came to me. A huge grin creased my face as, in my imagination, my ten-year-old self sat front and center on my lap for the rest of the evening, my loving arms around her waist.

The next day, I was to give my Soul to Soul Parenting talk at two breakout sessions. Feeling calm and even elated at the opportunity of sharing my perspective and contributing to the world at large, I opened my talk by acknowledging and praising the other presentations for their incredible new facts on brain research, along with the data on social and emotional learning. I expressed how the videos and Power Points were so very informative. Then, having acknowledged all that had come before me, I proceeded to say, "If I may, I'm going to offer a different vantage point now, with no data, no research, and no Power Point presentation. I'm here to speak to your soul, and there are simply no mathematical calculations or research to back up what I have to share because the soul relies on inner feeling for its truth." Then I shared the story of my experience the previous evening, explaining, "I can only stand before you and open my heart to you, offering you what I've come to *feel*, a perspective that moves from the inside out. If you can feel a resonance of what I'm sharing deep within you, perhaps through sensations in your body and a fluttering in your heart, you'll know whether it's truth *for you*. If you feel nothing, that's also a wonderful truth *for you*."

When I got into my car at the end of the day, I again saw myself back at age ten, smiled at myself, and thanked myself profusely for my courage and my wisdom. In a way I couldn't back then, I could now simply be myself—and there's nothing more liberating or empowering than that. My project was good enough, and so am I.

Degree or No Degree—We Decide

I have contemplated the idea of "the degree" a lot over the past several years. Is there a degree for much of what many of us desire to offer through our work today? In this age of technology and expanding paradigms, can we simply share our perspective and experience without the need to validate what we know by having somebody else label us as knowing it?

I'm not so much talking about a college degree as referring more to a degree in the abstract sense. Many don't go after their dreams because somebody hasn't awarded them a stamp of approval, attesting that they indeed are capable in their chosen field. While there are many careers in which a degree is necessary—an engineer, an allopathic doctor, an accountant, a veterinarian—more and more I'm sensing as I work with others on soul purpose that rather than seeking a degree for certain paths, we need to empower ourselves to walk through our own natural gateways. In many cases there's no formal qualification available for what we desire to do, and to feel we need one diminishes the message we espouse. In such cases we must be willing to create from our own personal truth, soul perspective, and life experience without apology. How do you award a degree for what makes your heart sing and your cells quicken?

In my case, I declared myself to be a soul nurturer, for which there is definitely no degree. Why? Because I knew myself, in my deepest space, to be one. I next declared myself a public speaker, though I hadn't taken a single class on public speaking but simply felt called from the inside to do it. Following on from this, I declared myself a Soul to Soul Circle creator and leader. While I formerly taught fourth and fifth grades and knew I had it in me to teach, there was no manual on how to effectively open a soul path for others in a group setting. Onward still, despite having never taken a specific creative writing or journalism class, I chose to become an author and a blogger. While I had no idea of the "rules," I allowed myself to grow *with* my writing as I went. Finally, broadcasting had never even crossed my mind until my publicist recommended radio. However, when the opportunity arose to try it, I felt an affirmation in my soul, once again learning as I went.

Perhaps we place too much importance on needing proof, research, data, external validation. These all speak to the mind and have their place, but sometimes we must decide from the heart. We are all messengers through *our lives lived*. We don't need a degree to share ourselves with the world. Not possessing a qualification should in no way cause us to feel diminished.

Facebook Envy

A recent study led by two universities in Germany found that many individuals feel diminished after visiting Facebook. Perhaps such individuals should decide that being made to feel this way isn't worth a romp with Facebook. On the other hand, this could be an opportunity for some good ole self-exploration. Seen in this light, social media is just the ramped-up juice we've been awaiting to bring aspects of our shadow to the surface so that we can get on with living from soul rather than from a wounded ego.

If you are one who often finds yourself envious, angry, sad, judgmental, and generally unhappy after a visit with your cyber friends, I suggest coming at social media from a different perspective. Get yourself a notebook, a pen, and an open heart, and each time you go on a site such as Facebook, commit to using it as a vehicle for your development into a whole person. Whenever you read a post and feel in your body—heart, stomach, throat—a tightening, make a note of it. Write down the trigger. Record how it made you feel. Begin to recognize the patterns. If you do this, you'll quickly discover that your angst has absolutely nothing to do with the individual who posted. Your diminishment isn't connected with their vacation, promotion, political view, or an event in which you weren't included. Rather, it has everything to do with your emotional landscape. If you are pricked by it, then it's yours to own and uncover all the way down to its roots.

For some of us it's enough simply to shed light on the theme and train ourselves to recognize it and let go of it the minute we feel it coming on. For others, the work of releasing a life theme may go more smoothly with outside help.

Social media—Facebook frenzy— is certainly not going anywhere, and it's *always* our choice to partake or pass. If we choose to pass, hopefully it's not because we're afraid to look too closely at ourselves, but because we truly aren't drawn to this particular medium of interaction. If we choose to participate, it's important to ensure we are *using it* rather than allowing it to use us. It needs to enhance, not cause us to feel diminished.

SHIFT
#12

From Resisting the Paradoxes to Resting Within Them

FROM ONE PERSPECTIVE TO MANY
FROM EITHER-OR TO BOTH-AND
FROM HIGHS AND LOWS TO EQUANIMITY
FROM JUDGMENT TO OBSERVATION
FROM ANXIETY TO GRATITUDE
FROM LABELING TO NEUTRALITY

The enlightened person is capable of perceiving both unity and multiplicity without the least contradiction between them.
HUANG PO

Are you able to be comfortable with contradictions? Can you embrace life's ambiguities, not to mention your own ambivalence? In other words, can you embrace life's paradoxes?

To make this shift, we can't be "plugged into" life in quite the same way as most are, by which I mean we have to become comfortable with experiencing life moment by moment, with all of its ups and downs, allowing it to flow wherever and however without resisting.

This shift requires us to move from judging to observing, from labeling to neutrality, and from anxiety to gratitude. We rise above duality into a new space that includes opposing vantage points. Indeed, we include all vantage points in a circle of compassion, understanding, appreciation, and oneness. This is what it means to be "in the world but not of it."

Different pasts—unique soul histories—create individual perspectives. In other words, our vantage point in large measure determines what we believe to be true. As the saying goes, "It depends on how you look at it."

Individuals can't be forced into this inclusive approach. It develops over time as our understanding of reality grows. Opinions and specific positions, while they might not totally disappear, often become less insistent. Dichotomies become delicious rather than being categorized as "morally bankrupt." Shades of grey abound.

Rethinking the Sacred

Nothing is exciting me more right now, personally or professionally, than the conscious blending of the profane and the profound, the sacrilegious and the sacred, the blasphemous and the spiritual, the earthy and soul. They may seem contradictory to many, and at one time appeared that way to me. But I came to see that the secular and the sacred are one and the same.

As a child, I was both the deepest and silliest member of our family—a walking paradox in many ways. Talking about God one minute and quick as lightening moving into discussing all things bodily (penis, balls, vagina—you get the picture). Then right back to lamenting disparities in our world and what to do about them.

There was my serious love of dance and a willingness to cut it up *loudly,* always loudly, anywhere, anytime, and in front of anyone. Then as I grew older, I slowly began to hide different aspects of myself. At first I hid the deeper, spiritual part from all but a few safe individuals, mostly non-family. Even as my self-exploration began literally enveloping my insides in extraordinary waves of deepened understanding and love, it wasn't until my early thirties that I felt comfortable enough to "come out" as Annie with my absolute love of soul.

Paradoxically, after I came out professionally as a soul nurturer, I hid publicly my more earthy aspects, which are also very much who I am, because I felt it might not be "appropriate" to show certain people *that* side of me now that I'd claimed my spot as a spiritual teacher.

The truth is, I'm a blended being and damned proud to be *all* of it. I'm ready to express *all* sides of myself to the world, for I've found there's no other path to freedom. Being fully and unabashedly ourselves is the only way to become whole—the consequence of which is that I'm risqué and saintly, sexual and pure, silly and deep, loud and quiet, profane and profound, ordinary and extraordinary.

I love a down-to-earth blog by a friend who recently wrote a particularly good one on teaching her children about Delores the Clitoris, and how she lovingly and humorously introduced her children to this awesome female body part. Yep, we speak that language in our family. And I appreciate blogs on spiritual development that invite self-love in a more esoteric way. We speak that language in our home too.

Today I desire wholeness for myself and others. I don't want to be boxed into showing only one side of myself to the world. I want to see all of you, and I want you to see all of me—no parts hidden away due to shame. I'm in love with the contradictions, the paradoxes, the dichotomies, and the opposites of life. Oneness includes *everything*—the good and the bad, the ups and the downs, the tidy and the messy, the earthy and soul. The lasting *peace* and the unconditional love we all desire come from embracing this larger perspective, rather than labeling and categorizing life as if it were separate *pieces*.

Utilizing the News to Expand Perspective

How I love my Chicago Tribune! I peruse it every morning and actually feel a wee bit unhinged if for some reason, like the other morning, it isn't waiting on my lawn as I do my dawn shuffle to the front door. On weekend mornings especially, I excitedly (and quite loudly, according to my family) extrapolate on articles in the paper. My excitement and vehemence typically come not from "Can you believe what this bastard wrote?" but from "Holy Moly, I perceived an issue in this way and now I see *more*."

While many may see the news as a downer that leaves them feeling overwhelmed or saddened, I've trained myself to search out the opportunities for an expansion of my perspective and to celebrate the news as a means to see aspects of life from a different vantage point. It's often the paradoxes and contradictions of the human condition that satisfy me the most. I enjoy seeking out the dichotomies in a story because I've come to know life as one giant and blessed dichotomy—seemingly opposite truths that share the same space simultaneously.

At first unknowingly and now quite consciously, my newspaper for the past twenty years has provided me with a daily practice of acquiring peace in the paradox, which represents much of the inner work of my journey. Some may feel that moving towards neutrality and equanimity might elicit a dullness, but this hasn't been my experience. Most of us live our lives somewhere between high surges and low drops that result from external events. With awakening, the fluctuation is less dramatic and more infrequent. This neutrality isn't at all similar to dullness. Quite the opposite, it's a vibrant aliveness, a peaceful presence, an active stillness, an inherent gratitude, and a sacred awe. From my perspective there's no high of ego that can top it.

Paradoxically, silliness and spontaneity increase as we liberate our soul. Undergirding our enthusiasm is a steady, contented feeling of well-being that remains *no matter what*. Similarly, sad experiences may cause us to moan and cry, but all the while we recognize that our fundamental "joy of being" isn't threatened.

To illustrate how a news item tends to broaden my perspective, some time ago Lonnae O'Neal Parker wrote about how the nation's feminists were divided over First Lady Michelle Obama calling herself Mom in Chief and focusing on growing vegetables and exercise rather than using her former career orientation to set an example for women. It turns out that many African-American women feel that a stay-at-home mom for a First Lady is a sign of progress. For me, the perspective broadener came as the article detailed how, throughout most of our American democracy, countless black women have had to work outside the home, often caring for children other than their own and cleaning another's home. Michelle Obama therefore represents a longed-for value. While many white women have been involved in the Mommy Wars debate, we tend to miss the fact it was a privilege to be able to debate the topic at all.

Time and time again I used to find myself beginning to judge something or someone as good or bad, right or wrong, disappointing or positive. But I found that when I took an either-or perspective, my stress level increased. In contrast, if I moved in the direction of both-and, my sense of peace increased. For me this proved to be a game changer. I learned we can unstick ourselves in many situations, not least relationships, by moving even a few steps closer to an acceptance of multiple perspectives. To take such steps is a natural outcome of becoming aware of the oneness that underlies everything.

The Sacredness of the Ordinary

Driving my daughter home from a hair appointment, I was overcome with what I call my "divine flow" energy feeling, which is characterized by breathlessness, a sense of heightened cellular activity throughout my body, moist eyes, and intense joy. Why did this feeling overtake me during this drive home? Simply because even the most mundane moments are shot through with luminosity when experienced through presence.

We don't have to wait for a mountaintop epiphany or an ashram retreat to pierce the sacred veil. The divine paradox is that once we pierce it, we arrive at the laughable realization *there was no veil in the first place!* Then books, movies, articles, songs, confrontations, illnesses, driving, and even laundry create the tapestry of a sacred life.

When we forego the judging and labeling of everything in life as either good or bad and remain in a more neutral position, the sacredness then shines through even those things we've been taught are anything but sacred. Indeed, to see the sacred in *all* of life, not just what we deem the best parts of life, is what awakening is all about. Which is why it's accessible to each and every one of us, dirty socks and all, not reserved for a chosen few.

Dirty socks, huh? Let me give you a few more images of how paradoxical and often downright contradictory living a sacred life looks like, on this occasion from the perspective of a mom. Lots of blogging moms these days talk about the dark side of motherhood. Utilizing colorful language, they discuss all things personal. I'd like to discuss a few of my own. Call them the gifts I wish to receive for Mother's Day.

I'll start with a month of never having to drag myself

off the couch and away from my favorite show to pick up yet another carpool of sweaty kids, *and* the opportunity to drive my wonderful children and their friends around forever. Next on my wish list, anyone—*anyone* besides me—to feed and walk our matted, bad-breathed dog, *and* the opportunity to walk and feed my sweet little pooch forever. Ah, and thinking of things stinky and in need of a wash, a laundress to cycle the ten loads of mucky socks and dirty drawers each week, *and* the opportunity to launder my beloved children's and husband's clothes forever.

Done with the sweaty stuff, how about a year without packing one more lunch before I've brushed my teeth or had my coffee, *and* the opportunity to feed my healthy children well forever? To which I'd like to add a kids-free vacation during which I can chill with my husband in *all* the ways that we love to chill, *and* the opportunity to vacation with my whole fun family forever. Along with that, I wouldn't mind a break from attending so many sometimes tedious youth sporting events while sitting on hard bleachers, *and* the opportunity to watch my sweet kids play sports forever. Topped off, of course, with a chance to sleep in on the weekends and awaken to make *only* my own breakfast, *and* the opportunity to make chocolate chip pancakes for a full table forever.

Did I say done with the sweaty stuff a paragraph ago? Not quite. For I could also wish for a house full of tidy rooms with no wet towels rotting on the floor, *and* the opportunity to peer into my kids' messy lived-in rooms forever.

Those trips to the stores for the family menu can get wearying, so for Mother's Day I would enjoy a year of small, easy grocery runs of mostly salad fixings, dark chocolate, wine and cheese, *and* the opportunity to fill grocery carts to the brim with all kinds of yum weekly forever. Along with the lighter shopping loads, I'd like time to focus on only *my* work, interests, and passions each day, without an endless annoying chore list, *and* the opportunity to share my life intimately with my children in close quarters forever.

Do you begin to see what sacredness is all about? It's simply becoming aware of *all* we are feeling, experiencing, *all* of the time, no matter how paradoxical something may be. It isn't "unspiritual" to not feel like doing that load of laundry, while at the same time loving the family for which you do it. Soul is about recognizing *everything* that's going on both within us and around us. It's this "awake" quality, which owns the whole of our life, that makes the secular sacred.

Experiencing the Sacred in a Grocery Store

Remember in our twenties, when the grocery store seemed the perfect place to meet your soulmate? Well, times have sure changed for me. Now a regular old trip to the supermarket provides an optimal opportunity for a full-blown ecstatic experience—seriously. I'm referring to a kind of "out-of-body" experience. While shopping at my local grocery store, I often have mystical moments—deep feelings of connection with the deli counter server, the produce man, and the bagger.

While it's true that grocery shopping isn't typically at the top of my list as a rip-roaring ball of fun, as I enter the store in purposeful surrender and gratitude for both the need to feed my family and the ability to do so, I open myself to the magnificent current of life found there and everywhere.

On this particular occasion, which some might label a psychotic episode but I see as often the best part of any day no matter where it occurs, I chatted with the cashier and observed him closely. What I perceived triggered a tingly sensation across the top of my scalp, breathlessness in my chest area, and tears in my eyes—not because I felt pity for someone having to do what may appear to many people to be a mundane job, but because I felt in the energy between us a timeless place in which we are eternally connected.

In the here and now behind our physical masks, it can be difficult to detect the true oneness that underlies all of life, yet this type of "paranormal" perception is indeed possible for each and every one of us—and not only in *Eat, Pray, Love*-style, but as a natural occurrence in our everyday reality.

More and more, people desire some type of personal spiritual practice as a treasured aspect of their week—meditation, gong baths, workshops, yoga—all fantastic gateways to the divine; for many, these are unrealistic activities on any regular basis in their normal day. Sure, an hour and a half in the "downward dog" can open us to a larger perspective. The problem is that as we move away from the yoga mat, we tend to lose the feeling of calm—especially when we have to grocery shop next.

This is where the insight that the true path is ultimately no path, but simply our life lived consciously, comes in. The experience of soul isn't reserved for specific endeavors that society deems elevated in some way. Rather, our spiritual practice becomes our way of being in the world—towards ourselves, others, and life in general. In other words, as we've touched on before, there's actually no mountaintop to climb, just a typical neighborhood street with its grocery store to savor and delight in.

While everyday life can sometimes seem status quo at best and downright drab at worst, the inner experience of it can shine light into even the darkest corner. If we can see what lies right in front of our noses beyond the surface first glance, a shiny world becomes readily apparent—even while standing in line at our local grocery store…and even in a long line at the post office during the holidays. (By the way, if you can pull off feeling the oneness there, give me a call, because you have just stepped into true master status!)

It's having our inner and outer eyes open that gives each moment an "eternal" quality, in that we are so fully immersed in it—so totally present—that it's *all there is* at that particular moment.

As Neale Donald Walsch expressed to me years ago, the message of the masters isn't that we *will* have eternal life, but that we *do*. We begin living it with the simple opening of our eyes to the sacred in the ordinary.

SHIFT
#13

From the Little Love to the Big Love

FROM ROLE TO ROLE TO SOUL TO SOUL
FROM JUDGMENT TO COMPASSION
FROM NON-FORGIVENESS TO LOVING THEM ANYWAY
FROM CLOSED HEART TO OPEN HEART
FROM HARDNESS TO SOFTNESS

The problem with the world is that we draw the circle of our family too small.
MOTHER TERESA

There are well over seven billion faces of the oneness on our planet, which means that in a sense there's only one of us here. As we become increasingly aware of this oneness, we leave the role-to-role aspect of relationship on the periphery and shift to navigating the world from a soul-to-soul perspective. Since role has usually taken center stage, this is a reversal of how we've always done things. What I call the "big love" now houses our integrity and is factored into all our choices. Soul connection becomes the determining factor in every interaction.

From the perspective of the big love, challenges arrive on our doorstep to provide optimal opportunities for development for all involved. When navigated with an open heart—a softness of soul—those on the "opposing" side in such challenges are approached from the perspective of oneness. Don't misunderstand and imagine the big love involves baring our soul to everyone we meet or always placing others' needs ahead of our own—and it's emphatically not about having poor boundaries or becoming a doormat. On the contrary, it requires us to speak our truth at all costs. With our boundaries intact, we do the things that are most natural for anyone who is aware of the oneness: we love those who make our lives difficult. As we increasingly wake up with love in our heart as a habit, to love the difficult person is felt as quite natural.

It's the *feeling* of an energy exchange that matters, whether it occurs at the Daytona 500, in the boardroom, in a monastery, or at a PTA meeting. When we understand that all action on the part of others stems from a belief that on some level justifies it as *right*, which is determined by the unique lens through which an individual views the world, we can more easily feel the oneness that binds us.

For example, a burglar who robs another to feed their family has allowed the inherent belief that they must take care of their family to trump the sense that it's wrong to steal from another. A soul-to-soul perspective takes in all angles of such a situation—the desperation in one party and the anger in the other. In such a case, the big love invites us to relinquish judgment and trust natural consequences to play out in purposeful ways. Even while perhaps acting to see that justice is indeed served, our sense of oneness never wanes, for the big love trumps all.

As the big love fills the visceral feeling space, we recognize that the real situation isn't one of parent to child, teacher to student, lawyer to client, doctor to patient, cashier to customer, or neighbor to neighbor, but soul to soul. When we see the soul first and the role second, we create a spaciousness within the interaction that allows for a greater possibility for the flourishing of love, compassion, nurturing, forgiveness, joy, and authenticity.

Seeing everyone as part of the oneness took a little getting used to, I admit. Initially I would sit in my car in the preschool pick-up line, relax on a bench at the park, or walk through the grocery store and purposefully view *every* individual who walked past me as a divine soul. As I did so, ordinary human beings began to appear differently to me.

Experiencing the Big Love

It was a picture-perfect afternoon, and after a morning of work and house busyness, I took off on my bike along Lake Michigan to walk one of my favorite beaches in Chicago and sit on a bench facing the crystal clear lake. The waves were rolling in with that feel of eternal change and motion that's so calming to the soul.

On the street leading to the beach, a crew was working on a sidewalk with jackhammers. My first thought was, "There goes my quiet." But as I passed them, I stopped my bike and sat for a moment observing this crew at work. Instead of being irked, I felt myself move into appreciation for their willingness to do a job that most take for granted. Everyone loves a fresh sidewalk or road, but who really wants to be standing on a loud jackhammer day in and day out?

As I watched, I noticed these men smiling and laughing with one another. They seemed relaxed and jovial. Seeing them perform their task with such ease, I too felt at ease and marveled at the myriad of ways in which human beings spend their days. So many different paths, each with their own challenges and pleasures—an infinite number of possibilities to experience physicality and evolve as a soul.

Eventually I went on down to the beach and had myself a glorious walk before settling on my bench. A few minutes later, I noticed that it was quiet. The crew was on a break, and one of the men walked down and stood a few feet from me. I watched as he took out a cigarette and began to stare at those breathtaking waves. Seeming lost in his own reverie, he stood there for a long time in silence and stillness, except for the hand going up to his mouth every now and then. I wondered about his life, his dreams, his family, and his interior world.

Suddenly, I felt tears well up as I dropped into that soul-to-soul space of oneness. From the outside, we appeared to be so different—age-wise, gender-wise, ethnicity-wise, and presumably economic-wise. Yet I felt such a deep sense of oneness with this man. I wasn't interested in the labels and the details, but simply felt a kinship with another courageous soul who had taken on the difficult task of being human. As we shared space and time, both experiencing the exquisite beauty of our physical landscape, all else faded away.

He eventually went back to work, and I got back on my bike for the ride home so that I could greet my children after school, drive them to practices, and make dinner. However, the moment with the man with the jackhammer has stayed with me. We pass by souls all day long. Do we see their beauty? Do we feel their presence? Do we understand who they are behind the physical mask?

Senator Rob Portman and The Big Love

So much in the news today makes me reflect upon the difference between the big love and the little love. Yes, love is love, although for most of us there tends to be more of the little love, which is reserved for a select few.

We have been conditioned to offer the little love to family, friends, and those who agree with us. In contrast, the spiritual "masters" refer to a love that doesn't stem from attachment and ownership. In the big love, the oneness, *everyone* is our own kind. Kinship is based on a shared divine essence. Love is soul to soul and all-inclusive.

When Senator Rob Portman evolved in his stance on gay marriage, as he sought to ensure his own gay son would have equal rights, he exemplified the way in which so many of us are bound to the little love rather than the big love. While I empathize with what I'm sure was an extremely difficult and raw experience for the Portman family, awareness of oneness invites us to move beyond our limited attachments and possessive inclinations to a vast eternal perspective. It's *this* perspective that will shift the way we treat others on this planet—changing our politics, economics, and education.

Our culture touts a mother bear stance toward our families. But how about a viewpoint that includes all? Yes, our child deserves our focus and protection, but can we also be available to the big love that encompasses all others? Martin Luther King, Gandhi, Jesus, Mother Teresa, Nelson Mandela, and many others are wonderful examples of what this might look like coming from an ordinary human being. However, we can no longer wait for a select few to offer the big love. Faced with the dangers of our technological era, it's no longer enough. We all must come to understand and embody the big love if we are to shift the disharmonious state of our world toward harmony. The big love needs to become the goal of all interactions, perceptions, and actions. Imagine a world in which our children were aware of and taught to tap into the big love above all else!

As adults, we must be willing to go first if we are to hold out any hope of raising conscious children who are awake to the big love. As Chameli Ardagh says in the book *Ordinary Women Extraordinary Wisdom*, "The Big Love serves the deeper space."

Valentine's Day—Let It Rip Your Heart Wide Open

The symbol of love in our culture is Valentine's Day. However, this needn't simply be a day to think of love only in terms of our own romantic partner or our own children or parents. Yes, Hallmark and Russell Stover want us to believe this is what a day that celebrates love is all about, but the big love points to something far grander.

The boy who answers you rudely in the carpool, can you love him anyway? The woman who bristles at you in the check-out line, can you love her anyway? The man who begs for money on the street, can you love him anyway? The woman who uses drugs, can you love her anyway? The girl who bullies your child, can you love her anyway? The husband who cheats, can you love him anyway? The mother who belittles you, can you love her anyway? The father who's weak, can you love him anyway? The murderer who endangers your family, can you love him anyway?

Loving such people "anyway" has nothing to do with intervening to prevent natural consequences from unfolding. To put this in street terms, if you do the crime, you do the time. Yet there's a heart-based perspective few on our planet seem to tap into—though a rare number have offered us this perspective and the message has always been "judge not" and the need to embrace "the peace that passes understanding."

From this big love perspective, we truly *see* a woman who has been abused. But likewise we truly *see* the man who abused her. We feel her pain, and we feel his rage. Then instead of judging, we love both. We see past the surface inhumanity and into the soul. It's this love that the world needs now, far more than it needs the limited love symbolized by Valentine's Day.

Rip your heart open wider, deeper, higher. All our hearts await the rip. Our world awaits seven billion rips.

Saying Goodbye to My Grocery Store

My local grocery store, one of a chain in the Chicago area, closed its doors along with all the other stores that bear its name. The parent company decided to let them all go due to insolvency. The store sits mere blocks from my home, and I shopped weekly at this particular location for almost twenty years—my entire married life.

It wasn't a Whole Foods or a Fresh Market—more of your standard large supermarket. But there was a familiarity, a warmth, and a sense of community I enjoyed—not to mention knowing the layout like the back of my hand. So when I first heard the news, I felt disappointed. The feeling of loss wasn't so much for the physical store itself, but rather the loss of all of the produce clerks, the cashiers, the baggers, the shelf stockers, the deli counter servers, many of whom had worked at the store for as long as I'd been shopping there. I had come to know these individuals and appreciated my interactions with them each week. I knew their names, about their families, and some of their passions and hobbies. I knew who walked in my neighborhood during his lunch break.

The point is that relationships had been created—a weekly and sometimes bi-weekly bond, formed in spite of the glare of harsh grocery store lights and often crowded food aisles. We shared many soul-to-soul moments.

The store that was to replace my store was under no obligation to keep these longtime employees, many of whom shared with me that after 39 years, 25 years, or 15 years, their pay was most likely too large for them to be hired by the new company. As they headed into the holiday season, their fates were unknown. So not only was there a feeling of loss on their part, but a financial fear weighing on their minds.

What struck me was that there they all were, each new day in a quickly fading job, exuding the same friendly demeanor. No matter what they may have been feeling inside, they were dispersing the big love to whatever degree they experienced it.

Loving the Person Who Violates Our Boundaries

I want to end our discussion of this shift with a practical illustration of how to move through feeling violated in a situation, so that we are able to understand why something happened and then enter into a state of compassion.

Our 2010 Honda CRV was stolen from the front of our home. It happened because of a situation I created. As we headed out to a baseball game and dinner with friends, I insisted we change cars so that we could enjoy our top-down soul bug. My husband already had keys to the other car in his hand, so we placed them in the drink holder once inside the soul bug. The night ended up being rather chilly, and I was in a sundress freezing my ass off wishing we had stuck with the Honda. Arriving home, we pulled into our detached garage on an alley, leaving the top down in the garage as usual. The inner door to the garage in our fenced yard always remains unlocked so that family members can easily go in and out.

In the middle of the night, three of the four of us found ourselves awake at 2 a.m. searching for water and using the bathroom, a total rarity. Our older daughter later awakened us with an early morning call to announce she had landed safely at JFK after a month in Thailand. It was then that I realized our car was gone. We discovered the bug had been rummaged through, which is how the thief gained access to the Honda keys.

Feeling violated is painful. No matter how much we may understand and deeply feel the truth of oneness, from a human perspective boundaries are important. Simultaneous awareness of the micro-lens and the macro-lens doesn't come easily in such a situation, particularly something like physical abuse, let alone a rape or murder. We must work through the self-love to get to the place where we can feel the big love in such a situation. Thankfully, we were only dealing with the loss of a vehicle, which was difficult enough.

For a car worth more than you can afford to lose, comprehensive insurance is a good choice. About four months before this event, with a new teen driver and high rates, we had switched car insurance companies to save money. I had also decided to remove the comprehensive cover on both cars, thinking we could easily afford to fix a broken windshield and were unlikely to experience theft of a car in such a wonderful neighborhood. Hence we weren't covered for this type of loss. As the implications of this realization dawned on us, the big love certainly wasn't what either of us was feeling.

In one of my Soul to Soul Circles we were discussing sustained neutrality as a hallmark of an awakened individual, and a lovely soul had a flash of a couple whom she has known since she was a young girl. Even as a child, she realized they responded to life's ups and the downs differently from most. They took the approach of, "How about that!" Even when their kitchen was flooded by a burst pipe, this was their response. It didn't mean they didn't take action, only that they didn't fight reality. What good would it do, since the flooded kitchen had already occurred? Resistance to what *is* leads only to mental torment, which merely compounds the problem. So…you missed your flight. How about that!

In the days that followed the theft of our car, we noted the ways in which we had made choices that created an opening for this type of violation. This was an act of self-love, since we were clarifying and fortifying our boundaries. Not that we deserved the theft, but on some level we recognized we called it forth from the sea of infinite possibilities. We both felt foolish and realized that much of the recovery work would involve our own self-forgiveness. We also discovered that, when faced with the ups and downs of life, "How about that!" is a powerful way to take a step toward the big love.

Having said this, I want to stress yet again that, as human beings, it usually requires a period of adjustment when a disappointment, major inconvenience, or devastation occurs. Every life has its ups and downs. Just because we become more self-aware—privy to the larger perspective of individuation within the oneness—doesn't mean we become immune to human challenges. It's okay if we don't instantly feel the big love for whoever violated us.

As I reflected more deeply on the theft, I became acutely aware of the fact that many are desperate as a result of the huge disparity between the haves and have-nots. While it isn't anyone's right to take from another without permission, I found myself understanding the rage and desperation that sometimes cause a person to do so. Instead of sowing bitterness in my heart, the stolen car increased my desire to speak out for greater economic justice for all. The big love was kicking in.

The incident also heightened our family's appreciation for our bountiful blessings. Our beautiful daughter was returning safely to us on that very day after a life-changing experience in Thailand. Gratitude abounded even as the possible financial loss sank in—even though the cost of replacing the car came close to one of our soon-to-be college student's annual tuition. Along with our gratitude for what we had, we needed to be more responsible and decided that a little more caution, though not fear and paranoia, would be a good thing. No more doors left unlocked, and new keypad locks on our garage and backdoor.

When you realize through loss what a gift something actually was, it's as if you begin to see it everywhere. I cannot tell you how many exact replicas of our stolen car we saw on the road in the two weeks before she was found, eliciting within us exclamations of, "Yep, she was a wonderful little car. How blessed we were to afford her."

Exactly two weeks after the event, we received a call from the detective letting us know our car had been located on the side of the road about twelve miles from our house. We got her back with minimal damage, and after a good detailing, drive her with greater care and appreciation.

We also purchased comprehensive insurance. It'll make it a little easier to feel the big love should loss of our vehicle ever surprise us again!

S H I F T
#14

From Individuation to Oneness

From Separation to Unification
From Literal to Multi-Dimensional
From Finite to Infinite
From Limited to Unlimited
From Duality to Non-Duality
From Death to No-Death

The fundamental delusion of humanity is to suppose that I am here and you are out there.
Yasutani Roshi

The man who stole our car was arrested for stealing another car that was found sitting, of all places, in front of his house! While this may sound like good news—another thief off the streets—it saddened me. This man lives in a neighborhood only a short distance from us in the city of Chicago, and yet we are light-years from him in terms of the realities of our everyday lives.

As with most large cities, Chicago is more like two cities within one. There are the more lovely, affluent areas, many with easy access to beautiful Lake Michigan and the stunning downtown. Then there are the "other" neighborhoods that have much more in common with Syria than my quaint North Shore village. Ironically, I had been reading to my family about the tragedies occurring within our own backyard, particularly within this specific neighborhood from which the thief hails. Because of the violence, it's an almost daily topic in the newspaper.

Last spring, one of our daughters participated in an eye-opening exchange with a large high school in the neighborhood in which this man was arrested. This led to honest conversations about the all-encompassing truth of oneness and non-dualism in the light of material differences and divisions, which can be so painful and at times leads to despair and even desperation in many of our fellow humans. Our daughter was absolutely astonished at the differences in education between peers from the two different schools, as well as the drastically different perspectives on life.

Out of curiosity, I looked at this man's Facebook page. As I suspected, on the surface our lives are nothing alike. It was as if we spoke different languages, almost like foreigners from distant lands. On the day after our car was stolen, his status update talked in colorful language about how he hoped it felt like s%$t to wake up in the morning and find our car gone, adding that he also hoped it cost a lot of money to replace.

It angered me to read such statements. I felt violated. So on the one hand I'm glad that he's being held responsible. Yet when I looked into this man's eyes in his pictures, and when I looked into the eyes of his baby and those of his recently killed brother in an RIP photo, I felt compassion and sadness for *all* of us.

We know not who we truly are, and this lack of remembering creates needless suffering that affects everyone. If we really knew, we wouldn't need a law to tell us "don't steal a car." We wouldn't need to be told "don't kill another." But then, no one would ever have a need to do such things because neither would we need laws to require that employees are paid at least a minimum wage. No one would be trying to pay anyone a bare minimum. Instead, we'd all be asking how *much* we can afford to pay instead of what the going rate is and how little we can get away with. Everyone would be able to live a dignified life because everyone would be coming from an internal knowing based on *felt* integrity instead of forced morality.

When I looked really closely at the man who stole our car and bragged about it to his friends, I felt his anger, his pain, and the poverty of his soul. And when I looked even closer, I saw myself. Because there's only one of us here.

Everything Is Part of the Oneness

Oneness is a state of being, not a set of beliefs. Everything we perceive carries within it the all-encompassing essence of everything, which is everywhere. It's rather like a holograph, in that all aspects of the whole exist in each individual part of the whole. So when sages from the past each in their own way encouraged people to follow The Golden Rule, treating others as we would ourselves wish to be treated, they weren't so much talking about what we refer to as "brotherly love," but were saying that we *are* the other and the other *is us*, because there's only one. This is quite different from brotherly love, and when such an understanding becomes embedded in our species it will change the world.

The fact that we are all part of a single reality doesn't call for sameness. On the contrary, the oneness invites us not to *suppress* our individuality but rather to *express* it in whatever way we choose. But though all individual expressions of the oneness are unique facets of the same diamond, and each called to express their facet in their own singular way, we always need to be aware that every individual expression affects the whole on some level, for the two can never be separate.

Initially it can be difficult to accept that everything is part of the oneness, even those things we deem wrong and the people who harm us. But as we embrace the fact that everything is sacred—including the most ugly, most deviant, and most incomprehensible aspects of humanness that arise from an unconscious mind—it transforms how we respond to everyone and everything. In the absolute realm of non-relativity, it cannot be otherwise. Unfortunately, many religions support separation thinking rather than oneness via their dogmatic exclusionary practices—an enigma, given that oneness can be found at the core of just about all the world's religions.

Speaking to my husband of oneness years ago, he commented that the oneness appeared to him much like a painting by Seurat. In pointillism, if we are near the painting, we can detect the individual dots that stand alone, while the whole painting can only be fully seen from further away. This has relevance for when a feeling of separation arises between ourselves and someone else. Even if we don't connect with certain human aspects of an individual (after all, we aren't all going to enjoy everyone equally), we may be able to connect with the shared oneness, which in turn alters our inner landscape toward them.

Near the end of my nine-month-long back struggle, having juiced the root cause and its many implications for all they were worth, I was driving in my Volkswagen Beetle convertible when the realization hit me that the neurosurgeon who wanted to operate on me was just as much in the oneness as any guru. It was the moment I knew for certain that oneness was to be my new reality through and through. As the initial waves of knowing subsided, it was as if my life passed before me and I was able to note all the misperceptions of separation whereby I had held certain relationships and life experiences in a dynamic of separation that wasn't real.

As my separation thinking collapsed, I came to realize that we are no closer to the oneness as a homemaker than as a monk, since there's no way to be closer to something that we *are*. It's simply a question of whether we are asleep or awake. Likewise we are no closer to the oneness as a victim than is the perpetrator—which is why I wanted to understand the circumstances of the man who took our car.

The Old Man in the Coffee Shop

I was to meet a woman for coffee to discuss our work, our passions, and how we might collaborate on projects close to our heart. It was a beautiful afternoon, and I whooshed into the bustling city cafe with red cheeks, my new hat, and generally brimming with life.

Since I had arrived several minutes before my new friend, I ordered my warm mug of coffee and took a seat, giving myself a few minutes to breathe in the vibe of the place—something I full-on love to do. I like to watch the people and feel the energy of a space. I find it fascinating and often quite moving to pick up on the subtle energies that can be felt in a new environment.

Once settled, I noticed an elderly man, kind of dressed up, sitting alone. He was likely a regular, as a few people said hello as they passed his table. Appearing shy, gentle, very worn-in, and maybe a bit out of place among the busyness of laptops and phones everywhere, he sat quietly drinking his coffee. Obviously on the tail end of his life, the contrast of where we both were on the linear timetable of the human life span struck me square in the heart. The opposite of what I thought I would feel while observing this beautiful man, I was awash with peace.

Suddenly the realization "he is me" came to me clear as a bell. Underneath it all, the core human experience is the same. In what will seem like the blink of an eye, I may be just blessed enough to be breathing, sitting alone in a coffee shop such as this, and appreciating the gift that has been my life. I was struck by the sacredness of it all, the awe of what it is to be a human being, and the tendency we all have to be oblivious to the beauty of it.

I wondered what this man was thinking and feeling as he sat there slowly sipping his coffee. What's it like to view the world from an aging vantage point? Does observing the youthful with full lives ahead of them bring sadness, regret, or perhaps appreciation and even relief? As my focus on what I might accomplish in my meeting with a new business acquaintance faded, I felt the fuller "me" through this old man. *What* I did during the second half of my life appeared rather insignificant. The only thing that seemed to matter was *how* I did it. Was it going to be marked by kindness, truth, compassion, openness, humor, and gratitude?

The only question really is how I might offer more love. If I honor this question in all I say and do, in a way that includes both myself and others, I will be able to sit in a cafe sipping my coffee without fear or regret. I'll feel the same peace I knew that day in the prime of my life in that coffee shop.

He is me. I am him. We are two individuated souls on the spectrum of the human experience, and when all is said and done, and there's nothing left to be stripped away, there's only the oneness. I felt it that day while observing an old man.

Life and Death Are Both Experiences of the Oneness

It isn't just in life that we are transformed by an awareness of oneness, but also during the experience of dying.

Several years ago, after hearing me speak at the local library, an acquaintance contacted me saying she had awakened in the middle of the night with a strong feeling I should visit her thirty-six-year-old brother-in-law who was terminal with pancreatic cancer. I reluctantly agreed, as at that time I hadn't worked with many terminally ill individuals. With my stomach in a knot, the following morning I headed to the hospital as a paid soul nurturer, not knowing my life was about to change.

The first visit was an hour and a half. While he was quiet and shy, and I was nervous, it felt like we had known each other for a long time. We talked of different aspects of his life, mostly the things he enjoyed, and of his tremendous fear of impending death. The conversation was gentle.

A few days later his sister-in-law called to say he had asked for another visit. This time I mostly just sat quietly with him and held his hand. This was my final paid visit. What followed were twenty-five more visits as simply his friend over a period of five months. I have never been the same since I moved past my fear and agreed to be fully present with a stranger during his experience of dying.

Opening to death has opened me to life. For a start, I learned we're all capable of caring for one another in deeper ways than we often allow, and we can all choose to offer more of ourselves. Since there's no separation in the oneness, it turns out that when we genuinely reach out to another, we ultimately reach into *ourselves*.

The surrender process takes time, but eventually the masks begin to fall away—often for both the dying and the soul nurturer, since dying offers an opportunity for much greater intimacy than we generally allow in life. To witness another surrender, watching as the personas and facades fade, is a beautiful gift. This man shared that he had actually never been so free to be himself during his active life as he was during these visits in which he was bedridden.

If there's ever an opportunity for sunlight, fresh air, and squirrels, take it. One of our most memorable visits, and the only time I ever saw this man out of bed, was on a beautiful spring day in Chicago. We enjoyed a slow walk together with him in his wheelchair, simply feeling the gift of life on Mother Earth. It was his last outing with blooming trees over his head, gentle breezes at his back, and the warmth of sunlight on his skin.

Ask the individual about their life, the ups and the downs of it. Ask about their feelings on death, including their fears and the possibility of release. Acknowledge the pain, fear, and sadness—and also acknowledge the grace, beauty, and peace, since these seemingly opposite feelings are on the same spectrum. Help the dying individual feel them all.

Both birth and death are the same doorway into and out of the human experience. It's nothing short of an immeasurable honor to be present for either. Be free to emanate appreciation, perhaps above any other feeling, in the presence of the dying individual. Allow yourself to feel whatever human emotions you are feeling, and at the same time remain connected to the larger perspective of oneness. Remove *your* masks and express love. With every touch, every look, every word, every action, offer love. Let compassion and tenderness for this beautiful soul overwhelm you.

As the death gets closer, open yourself to the light. It's strong, beautiful, and can be felt by the living who are awake to it. The same light that will envelop your loved one as they transition is available all the time, though acutely so during the death experience. Bathe yourself in this light. I have never felt anything more enticing. A few weeks before his death, my friend surrendered to the light. Consequently he stopped being afraid. The fight was over.

I was with my friend less than twenty-four hours before he passed. I knew it was close when I entered the room on my last visit. His eyes had changed, as had his breathing, and he seemed only part in the body now. There was nothing more to say, only a state of being to share. As he lay in a fetal position with almost nothing left on his bones, I kissed him on the cheek one last time and simply said, "Chris, thank you for making my day."

Barely opening his glossy eyes, he smiled almost imperceptibly and said softly, "Annie, thank you for making mine."

What a wonderful experience of oneness.

The Veil Is Thin

I was driving alone in my car listening to music after dropping a carload of kids off at a sports practice, when I began to think appreciatively of an individual who had recently made her transition from this life. I didn't know her well, having seen her a few times every summer over the past eighteen years up in the Northwoods of Wisconsin where our families both vacation. Although her husband had survived, she had passed in a car accident on her way home that last summer.

As I thought of her, thanking her for being kind and wishing her well on the next leg of her journey, suddenly it was as if her presence was in the car with me, her energy enveloping me in waves of love that moved throughout my body. Tears sprang to my eyes, my breathing became a loud breathlessness, my scalp experienced an alive tingly sensation, and I became literally immersed in oneness. A greater ecstasy I have never known. Then after several seconds the energy faded. Since that soul union, I have felt my beautiful friend, and many others, on the other side. The oneness we can experience in life doesn't end with death.

Not too long ago, I spent a weekend with close girlfriends in Chicago during which we laughed our way through several walks and restaurants. The week after, the father of one of my friends, who had passed at a young age several years before, came to my mind. I had known him growing up and really loved his warmth, generosity, and sense of humor. I opened a dialogue with him, letting him know what a wonderful mother, friend, and utterly lovely woman his daughter had become. Suddenly, his energy was with me in the same manner as that of the woman I knew in Wisconsin.

I mention these experiences, which leave me breathless with a feeling of "drop to my knees gratitude," because I want others to know that this type of soul union is possible for any who truly desire it. Once considered the prerogative of a select few, I now know these mystical experiences to be available to all.

Of course, one doesn't need to open to this type of soul union to be happy. But for me, expanding my capacity to feel beyond the earthly dimension has changed my life. Experiencing the eternalness of life generates awe at the sacredness of the journey. Once viewed from an aerial vantage point, there's no going back to seeing the world solely through a three-dimensional lens.

The first step to such experiences involves changing the way you see *yourself*. Do you see yourself as primarily a physical body and a personality that lives hopefully one full life span, then heaven evermore? Or do you see yourself—and all others—as a soul with a vast history and an infinite future that's part of an unimaginable divine presence that never dies?

How to create a relationship with those on the other side? Begin by announcing your willingness, readiness, openness, and pure desire to connect beyond form, soul to soul. You might want to use something like the following: "My dear mother who gave me life on the beautiful earth plane, I want you to know that I know you are there, and I'm ready to create a wholly (holy) expanded relationship with you. I invite you to connect with me regularly so I may feel your glorious presence. Show me signs. I am awake, and I will see, hear, and listen—not with my intellect, but with my heart and soul. Thank you, my beloved mother. I love you to infinity and beyond."

Practice soul to soul connection on the earth plane with other human beings. Increase moments of solitude, meditative time spent in nature, and time spent listening to uplifting music, since its vibration passes easily and purely through the veil. Especially when someone is about to leave this world, connect deeply with them if you can.

For instance, a friend of mine spoke openly to her mom about her life, her death, her feelings. She thanked her mom for all of it—the ups *and* the downs. The magnificence and glory of it all wasn't lost in the sadness of losing the woman who gave her birth. Of course, she felt the sadness; but she simultaneously felt the incredible beauty and profound joy. She affirmed that this wasn't the end, but rather the beginning of a new relationship in which they could always share through feelings and signs. My friend let her know she would be ready, willing, and able to continue an ongoing relationship with her at all times. As a token of their oneness, she invited her mother to remain a *felt* part of her life.

Teen's Suicide—A Call to Us All

My heart landed in my throat several years ago as I came upon an article about a teen suicide at Rutgers University, triggered by a thoughtless and downright unconscious webcast by two peers. It's unfathomable that such bias, ridicule, and homophobia still exist in society—still exist despite a growing awareness of our oneness.

While we are all on our own individual paths to enlightenment, the primitive behavior exhibited by these two students needs to be examined by all of us, since the collective consciousness of our culture as a whole is accountable for all of its members. How is it that we are raising children who can name the quarterback of every professional football team, the latest winner of American Idol, or the top video game on the market, yet who don't understand basic life-affirming principles in their dealings with others? How is it that we don't teach and promote awareness of our oneness?

There's a missing piece (peace) here that touches every aspect of our society—politics, economics, healthcare, religion, family life, and individual well-being. At an early age, children need to be introduced to the fact that there are countless valid paths, as well as no path, whether the path concerns religion, sexual orientation, politics, or any number of aspects of everyday life. We can offer a clear example of acceptance by releasing our own need to judge and instead seeing everyone through the lens of oneness.

A teen's suicide is often extremely complex, and this case was undoubtedly no exception. Yet it's society's monumental loss that one of our own—a gifted violinist, inviting others to know themselves more intimately through music—departed in such a way in part due to others' lack of clarity surrounding their *own* magnificence as blended beings and an awareness of their oneness with this peer. For once an understanding of our own nature as grounded in the oneness is uncovered, it becomes impossible not to see and feel the energetic connection that underlies the whole of life.

SHIFT
#15

From Physical Being to Blended Being

FROM COMPARTMENTALIZATION TO INTEGRATION
FROM SOCIETAL NORMS TO SOUL RESONANCE
FROM ANOTHER'S TRUTH TO OWN TRUTH
FROM UNCERTAINTY TO TRUST
FROM UNEASE TO GRATITUDE
FROM CONSTRAINTS TO FREEDOM
FROM EGO ORIENTATION TO CONSCIOUS SPIRIT EMBODIMENT
FROM HALF TO WHOLE

It is time for humanity to awaken at a collective level. Enlightenment can no longer be for just a select few, who no longer participate in the world. If there is to be an awakening at a collective level, we will have to learn to function within the world. This means that we will have to find a balance between the timelessness of the fully awakened state and the world of time.
LEONARD JACOBSON

Did you see the video, first aired on YouTube, of six teens beating another youth for shoes, a jacket, and money, while shouting racial slurs? The video is shocking, though all too familiar—and not just in America, but in societies around the world.

Following this tragedy there were the usual demands to "make our streets safer." Unfortunately, if we keep looking to the same outworn solutions, we will again come up empty-hearted. More police on the streets, anti-violent video game sympathy, and longer hours in school will ultimately do nothing to break down the anger, disillusionment, desperation, and outright loss of human feeling we see all around the globe.

What *will* make the difference is an awakening that's rippling through the hearts of humans on every continent. Though not yet mainstream, and often labeled as New Age by the media, it's the wave of the future. We are poised at a tipping point, where centuries of seed planting are beginning to come to fruition. Like-minded humans everywhere are gradually turning the tide of human degradation, uplifting not only individuals but institutions worldwide.

Faced with our many challenges, the usual band-aids are no longer working. Wars, morality-based laws, and restrictions on personal freedom are simply ineffective for addressing the complex issues of our day and no longer serve our species. As the traditional ways in which human beings relate collapse all over the planet, with nation after nation in uproar, institution after institution in the throes of change, an eventual *complete* overhaul of our ways of running our world will occur.

This shift, which over time will affect all aspects of societies around the globe, is at once both simple and complex. From a material perspective, for many the coming years will likely be at times uncomfortable, even painful. It will feel to many that societies as we have known them, and the institutions within them—economic, political, religious, cultural—are crumbling. Those who seek to hold onto the old views, the former ways of perceiving, the outdated style of doing things, will increasingly find their beliefs overturned.

We are all in this together, and nothing can change that. The growing pains of the new world that's emerging are inevitable, and we will all feel them. Going with the flow will make them bearable, whereas resistance can lead only to acute pain. Consider, for instance, the accelerating acceptance of gay people, the rise of women, the spread of democracy. The tide has turned, and it must be extremely painful for those who continue to see life as black and white, whose mentality is that others are wrong and they are right, who take the position of "my way or the highway." Those with such judgmental, ego-based mindsets are in for an increasingly rough ride. If they don't get onboard as their way of doing things is replaced, their lives will become hugely distressing.

For those with clear sight, there will be a recognition that the breakdowns are gradually precipitating breakthroughs, as the way we have done things becomes transparently bankrupt. Many of our present institutions will be seen for the irresponsible, ego-based, destructive systems they truly are. In their place will emerge more transparent, responsible, balanced, honest, and heart-centered ways of doing things that, rather than survivalist in nature, draw upon the oneness for their validity.

Clues abound that change is accelerating. Observing what's afoot through the lens of soul, one glimpses the light shining with growing brilliance through the darkness. Everywhere I look, I see people breaking free of the old stigmas, sending the former norms packing. There may still be great injustice in the workplace, for instance, but for millions the situation is a whole lot better than the 1700s, for example, when even kids of five worked up to eighteen-hour days in grimy conditions and were dead at a young age. True, there are still sweatshops, slavery, and trafficking of women on the planet, although consciousness of these oppressive practices is growing. Their days are numbered.

Love, forgiveness, non-judgment, transparency, wholeness, and a sense of oneness are available as never before on our planet. Those who refuse to live in the emerging consciousness of oneness, such as terrorists who seek to impose their old religious and societal codes, governments that oppress their people, and corporations that treat their labor unjustly, are on the losing side of history. All will ultimately awaken to the oneness that seeks to express itself everywhere.

We *Need* a "New Age"

I was on a local radio show recently and the minute I began speaking in terms of soul to soul and energy, the host dismissed me as New Age. Now, I can joke about myself as much as anyone, and I'm not afraid to admit to being a metaphysical gal. But today, it might do us all well not to deem another's ideas about how our world can become a loving planet as "out there." After all, nothing else has ever worked.

I can't tell you the number of times after giving a talk that I've been told, "Your message gave me goosebumps, brought tears to my eyes, and ignited a feeling of joy, but the schools and PTAs just aren't ready for this kind of soul-to-soul message." Really? Take a look at the video of the Chicago beating, then ask yourself: do we not desperately need a new era that has some *soul* to it?

I'm not talking about what most immediately think of when they hear the term "new age"—you know, peace signs, crystals, and rainbows. I'm talking about a shift in consciousness, whereby a society would never need laws to deter the beating, raping, or killing of another being like oneself. The rage, violence, and greed in our society aren't economic, religious, or political problems. They are a soul problem that's then reflected back to us in each of these areas of society.

The Dave Matthews Band, Wrigley Field, and Beyond

Beyond the booze and other substances on Wrigley Field this evening, upon looking *outward* to other beings swaying in unison, and peering *upward* to a vast sky, a larger perspective was available for all to experience—a perspective that's always available but often missed in the busyness of an ordinary day.

It happens every time I see the Dave Matthews Band onstage, offering their energy and passion up and out for others to capture within themselves the creative power that exists in all of us. I gain a renewed sense of my own self-realization as part of the oneness and therefore as a creator in my own right.

When I watch this band perform, I find them to be so comfortable in their own skin that it reignites in me a strong desire to live true, so that I may truly live. Emanating from a band who writes their own music and therefore fully own it on a soul level, the energy in these performances feels authentic. To see, and more importantly to *feel*, the vibration of another's uncensored energetic output is a gift, for in the largest sense we are all connected in an unseen yet deeply felt matrix that pulsates just beneath the surface of what we deem reality. Soul recognizes when another is offering from the same timeless well, and this recognition gives us permission to unleash our own potential to share ourselves with the world.

The call of the Dave Matthews Band experience isn't to idolize a group of human beings who have simply created a means to do what they love and love what they do, but to excavate our own extraordinary capacity to inspire heightened life experiences. From a vortex of self-love, creativity, joy, and empowerment, we are enabled to move toward our sacred potential. Whether it be as a musician or bar owner, teacher or hairdresser, how much uplifting of the human spirit are we willing to offer? As a famous individual once said, "The whole world is a stage." Whether your stage is in front of thousands or simply on your own front porch matters not. The key is to be yourself in the fullest sense. Such an offering is enough.

"You're SO Spiritual...Sorry for Cussing in Front of You"

A few years back when my older daughter was on a travel soccer team, reacting to a missed opportunity on goal, a parent at a soccer game cussed out loud. Instead of looking more closely at *herself* to understand her reaction to a mistake made on the field by a mere eighth grader enjoying a sport, she turned to me and joked in front of everyone, "Oops. Can I say that in front of you? I know you're *so* spiritual."

It's a common misperception that some of us are "spiritual," whereas others of us are more secular. Individuals who hold this misperception don't realize that we're all spiritual beings, whether we become conscious of it in life or through the death experience. Ironically, this woman had arrived at the tournament fresh from her daughter's confirmation that very morning! Apparently religion and spirituality mean two different things to some.

Spirituality, or living from soul as I prefer to say, involves becoming aware of often unnoticed aspects of reality, so that a whole new perspective becomes apparent. It can be difficult to explain this to someone who confuses spirituality with morality. To live from soul isn't about safeguarding a particular society's "moral" standards, but about living with integrity. As one's awareness increases, it becomes hard to live without integrity.

As a soul-oriented individual, I have no desire to judge another's choices. My heart's desire is for us all to look more closely at our *own* choices. So if cussing feels good to you, then have at it. Eventually that choice may or may not serve your higher good. If dancing on a tabletop feels good to you, then go for it. Eventually that choice may or may not serve your higher good. (I did so fairly recently and loved every minute of it, by the way.) If sitting in meditation for hours floats your boat, then enjoy it without apology. Eventually that choice may or may not serve your higher good.

The point is to come to know ourselves better. This we do by discovering our own deepest being, as we make choices and discover there are no "wrong" turns per se, and that the natural consequences of every choice are all a means of enabling us to know whether cussing, tabletop dancing, meditation, or anything else in life truly works for us. The blended being perspective encourages all to become so intimate with themselves that all can feel their way *energetically*. The sensitive inner compass then naturally moves all in the direction of authenticity, joy, love, gratitude, service, and empowerment.

Cuss, cater, or CEO your way to freedom. Bowl, bake, or bike your way to bliss. At every turn, *you* decide.

Falling in Love with Soul in All Its Humanity

While the past few shifts in particular have focused greatly on recognizing the soul aspect of the blended being perspective, I can't stress enough the importance of also recognizing the way soul expresses itself in our physicality. It's the interplay of both my deepest being and my earthiness, held in full consciousness, that fills me with undimmed joy. I call awareness of both aspects "the blended moment." The awe of the human condition begins here. Gratitude that wells up and out from deep inside begins here.

On a Friday evening, my husband and I were sitting at the bar of one of our favorite neighborhood restaurants enjoying appetizers, a few beers, and each other. This type of evening thrills me—simple and yet fulfilling. At one point I observed the bartender as he worked and chatted with patrons. I looked around at all the people in the restaurant, most of whom were eating, drinking, and laughing. Something about this ordinary Friday evening struck me as so beautiful. I felt an intense appreciation for our physicality, which allows for such a rich soul experience. I felt the oneness everywhere in the guise of people, strings of lights, and a textured mahogany bar. I shared my deeply felt appreciation with my husband, and he agreed.

Acknowledgment and appreciation for everyday humanness make our daily path extraordinary. As the self spirals upward into wholeness, shedding what's no longer needed of the cocoon of ego, our heart becomes enveloped in awareness of oneness, so that the earth expression of our soul, instead of being seen as contrary to our true being, is to be highly regarded and enjoyed.

I fell in love with my soul before I fell in love with the way it has chosen to express itself in my humanity. While it didn't take too long on the awakening journey to experience the soul-to-soul nature of relationships within the oneness, it took me much longer to accept and appreciate the human expressions. The opening occurred as I began to recognize the universal human traits within all of us—the light and the dark possibilities, which are turned on and off as a result of many factors such as past conditioning. It was by first seeing these traits within myself that I became aware of their universality and that we are connected in our shared humanity as well as in our ultimate oneness.

Awakening is about *consciously* enjoying the ride, which, if allowed, is a wild and glorious ride. A common deathbed regret is that the person didn't fully live. A set of beliefs or practices, often revolving around suffering and sacrifice, together with strict adherence to a rather narrow or at best middle-of-the-road existence, mars many a life. For the awakened person, a grocery store, baseball game, park bench, place of work, or pew in a place of worship all serve their soul.

Getting to this point is a corkscrew movement whereby the shifts discussed in this book come into view and deepen through experiences that create opportunities to unload our psychic debris. As we lose our dependence on the external world for our sense of worthiness, happiness, love, and empowerment, we begin to enjoy the external world in a way that simply wasn't possible as long as we were needy of it for an identity.

As a blended being we learn to tend our whole garden. In fact, we come to understand that we *are* the garden—the sun, the wind, the rain, the earth, the weeds, the flowers, the bees. Sitting on a park bench watching a family play—even if a fight breaks out between the two older children—is just as "spiritual" as chanting in a monastery. As I covered in an earlier chapter, the sacred and the sacrilegious, the profane and the profound, the messy and the clean all share the same space. To see the two as opposed creates an imagined separation that simply doesn't exist.

Initially this state of no separation between seeming opposites feels unsettling and a bit scary because it's being viewed through the wide eyes of a wet hatchling just out of the egg. At the same time, something about it feels like home. As the inner and outer worlds are bridged by full embodiment, we enjoy all that comes under the umbrella of this union. The gratitude that flows freely between us is direct and profound, for we know how dear we are to one another. We feel the connection and know without a doubt we are in this together. We experience it as one great love affair, affecting every nook and cranny of our existence.

I want to end this shift with a brief description of "The Prophecy of the Condor and the Eagle" of which most cultures offer some type of accounting. Basically, and in my own words, this prophecy states that eventually (around now in human existence) the condor with its more heartfelt, intuitive, and soulful nature, and the eagle with its more linear, cerebral and physical nature, while previously at odds with one another—the latter almost pushing the former to annihilation—will come together as "one" and enjoy the same sky.

While there are different levels on which we can interpret this prophecy, I think it provides a wonderful example of the blended-being experience that this book seeks to portray. The shift in consciousness is one that includes both the condor (soul) and the eagle (the physical). It is indeed time for these two aspects of ourselves to merge within so that we may fly as one blended being in the infinite sky of oneness.

Final Thoughts

*I looked in temples, churches and mosques.
But I found the Divine in my own heart.*
Rumi

There is in all visible things…a hidden wholeness.
Thomas Merton

It's not what you look at that matters, it's what you see.
Henry David Thoreau

I've often heard it said that there are three different stages of awakening. In the first stage, we come to know ourselves as a blended being and begin living as an embodied soul. In the second, we see everyone and everything as an expression of the ultimate oneness that underlies reality, which tends to awaken an intense love for humanity and a desire to be of service. In the third, which it's said few ever reach, our self seems to disappear altogether as we merge into the whole.

You're already interested, right? You want to know about that third stage. You see, the human mind loves mysteries. Naturally curious, it finds it tantalizing to try to imagine states that are somehow "beyond." But what if there is no mystery? What if there are no truly "advanced" masters who are just so much further on than us?

The question I wish to pose is whether the human mind is a reliable sounding device. Or could it be that the mind, which is so often tied up with ego, would prefer to avoid fully awakening in ordinary, everyday life, thereby delaying the final stage of actually becoming an expression of the oneness for some distant future, perhaps another lifetime?

If you've tracked with me this far in *From Role to Soul*, you know by now that the experience of manifesting the oneness isn't one in which we "disappear," but one in which we *show up* in all our magnificence. We don't merge *into* oblivion, but find ourselves increasingly self-expressing *from* an eternal and infinite wholeness. Through us, the oneness becomes incarnate in ordinary, everyday life.

It's the experience of being an individuated, unique expression of the oneness that the shifts I've outlined lead to. Offered here from my path, my vantage point, these shifts are simply a close-up of one possible direction with universal threads—that's all. I've shared them only to encourage you to trust in your own unique journey, have faith in your own direction, be true to who you are.

All paths are gifts, for they offer to each specific soul the particular joys and challenges that invite flourishing. We need our paths until we no longer need them. I want to emphasize that all paths, including no path, have ups, downs, and in-betweens. This doesn't change once we are living as a blended being. The challenges now simply include a consciousness that penetrates well beyond the mere surface of a human life. The only thing that has changed is our awareness of an indestructible connection to the oneness—now a constant companion. We continue to experience all aspects of an ordinary life, though perceived in a much different way. Whereas before we were unaware of an unwavering, still center, this inner well is now our greatest strength—unfathomable to those not yet aware of this source within them. Utter silence—the oneness itself—can be found there in its unexpressed form.

It's also important to understand that we don't require out-of-this-world mystical experiences to move forward on the awakening journey. Oneness, as felt through our own soul, is always present, not even a breath away. It's a state of bliss, which is fundamentally different from what we call "happiness," though it undergirds all our experiences of happiness. The difference is that it isn't dependent on anything exterior, such as a relationship or a situation working out well; rather, it consists of a certainty of being grounded more deeply than any external circumstances.

Basing our experiences on the more shamanic experiences of others would be misleading. The partnership created within a blended being is an internal one. The circumstances of our external life may or may not appear to be changed at all, other than priorities and choices exuding an underlying texture of oneness that can be perceived by others who are also in alignment with soul. Besides, although we are initially highly conscious of ourselves as a blended being, eventually it becomes so fully integrated as who we are that it's indiscernible.

Sometimes it isn't until a particular challenge shows up in our life that we recognize the extent of our development. The barometer is how effortlessly we can hold the entirety of life in our hands and heart.

The Message and the Messenger

Though the guru is always ourselves, there will be guideposts in our lives at moments. Some will be loud, full of life, charismatic. Others will be solitary, quiet, gentle souls. All human teachers are imperfect, which is why I feel our relationship only needs to be with the message, not necessarily the messenger. If we confuse the two and begin to follow the messenger rather than simply integrate, in our own way, a message that resonates, we'll likely end up disillusioned.

It's my great hope that a new paradigm of spiritual teaching is dawning, inviting soul-to-soul exchanges, companionship, and guru gatherings rather than the top-down model of teacher-student. The latter is where I think not only New Age models have failed, but traditional religion as well.

We must take full responsibility, in this and in all things, for identifying what feels true for us—nothing more and nothing less. If a message moves us, then the messenger has done his or her job. Greater intimacy with our own soul stems from working with the message, not the messenger.

Spiritual Activism and Service

I have come to realize that my overriding responsibility toward humanity, if there is indeed one, is not based on a specific action, but rather on an awakening from which all right action can stem. There is not a right amount of service. If we do choose to serve beyond simply being awake in our everyday life, we will know what acts of service our soul calls us to do. These acts will fulfill us as much as we will fulfill them.

Parenting

Many adults today must parent themselves right along with their children in a simultaneous fashion. As we learn to fly, we give our children permission to do the same. There is no greater gift that we can give our children than our own awakening. In this way we empower our children, our most important job as a parent.

Relationships

Our most important relationship is with our soul. Once this primary relationship is developed, then all other relationships will unfold in an authentic way. In relationship with another, wholeness is the key. It is of great value to determine whether or not the relationship is based on shadow aspects from either or both participants or the soul. We are not always privy to the soul purpose of relationships. Relationships of all stripes offer enormous awakening potential. There is no magic formula, only a commitment to self-love and soul to soul with others.

Problems in Our World

Death is a surefire way to experience oneness. But humanity evolves through our expressing oneness in everyday moments. Conscious soul-embodiment is possible for all.

There aren't as many problems in the world as we might imagine. There is instead one primary problem—not enough of us have awakened. Ultimately, *we choose* faith or fear, inclusion or exclusion, appreciation or disdain, acceptance or resistance, hope or despair. We choose truth or untruth, kindness or cruelty, equality or inequality, love or hate. We choose the peace that passes all understanding. We decide. We choose.

The Spiritual Bypass and Acedia

Sometimes after being on a spiritual path for many years, we come to a place of indifference where it seems that nothing really matters because, ultimately, all is well. While in the largest sense this is of course true, it can signal a dangerous slide into lethargy and depression. We can't bypass any of the stages of awakening. Too often, in the name of being "spiritual," many bypass their more earthy aspects rather than blending them with a soul perspective to lead an *active* life within the oneness. I have been in this place a few times, thinking that I was further along the awakening journey than I actually was. It's a trap.

During one of these periods, in a long conversation with a friend and colleague, she introduced me to the term "acedia." Acedia is a spiritual laziness or apathetic indifference that can occur at any time, but especially when we attempt to bypass our physicality for our spirituality. She shared that the term first came about because sometimes monks would become afflicted with this tendency. The prescription for restoration had to do with whether the monk was an introvert or an extrovert.

For example, if a monk typically spent time in a solitary fashion such as meditating or scrubbing floors, then the monk would be assigned different tasks that involved community, such as working in the kitchen or teaching. If the monk with acedia was currently involved in community-oriented pursuits, the opposite approach was recommended. These shifts were not necessarily meant to be long lasting, but long enough to break the acedia, giving rise to a more balanced life.

It's perhaps helpful to know that the shifts I've outlined may look and feel different for a person whose natural tendency is more extrovert (one who replenishes by being with others) than for the individual who's more of an introvert (one who replenishes by being alone). And maybe not. For when we awaken, some of us discover that our introversion or extroversion was merely a mask for our feelings of inadequacy, a way of hiding from who we really are.

Still, I want to honor people's individual tendencies. If you tend more toward introversion, it will be encouraging to know that monks and nuns have exemplified for centuries the value of quiet, solitude, simplicity, and still-

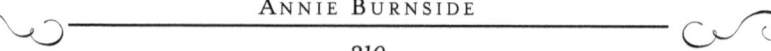

ness on the awakening journey. And if you're more extroverted, never has there been a time when communication is more readily available than it is today—as I pointed out from my experience with Facebook.

While it's true that our fast-paced era can be a detriment to awakening, the vast majority of us no doubt need both community *and* solitude in order to be whole. The degree to which each is established within our life should be a personal preference and isn't a prerequisite for awakening.

It's likely that extroverts find they need much more solitude, while introverts find they need more community. The point is that there needs to be a balance of introspection and outward expression, as well as action and non-action, offering and allowing, that feels appropriate for us. Neither one is a more admirable mode than the other.

It's also important to note that a blended being learns to "be" while doing—a hallmark of the self-realized state. Consequently all that's required is for each of us to know in our own soul what's needed in our particular case moment by moment and day by day. We must each feel our own way to wholeness.

A final comment about acedia. Paradoxically—as with so many things—when one awakens, the feeling of "it doesn't matter" does indeed rise to the surface, but not in a hopeless, uncaring way. Rather, it's simply an untethering from the need for life to unfold in a certain direction. One feels like freedom, while the other feels like hopelessness. "What's the point?" is fundamentally different from awareness.

There is of course a point to awakening, and a young woman expressed it accurately in an essay: "My generation has to confront the mass culture we have created and change it for the better. Our parents and grandparents demanded change, but through legislation. We won't be able to achieve the same kind of change. We have to confront popular culture, not politicians. The question that scares me is: how do you change a popular culture that has so much control over what your generation becomes?"

The young woman added, "The issues that plague our society aren't really legislative anymore. We can't really make that many more laws to deal with them. They're cultural. We can't demand they change the way we think. *We* have to do that."

Awakening is about just such a change—for ourselves, and for everybody on the planet. That's the point.

Appendix 1
A Self-Love Kit

Mental health is such an important topic in these times, as culturally we face a worldwide epidemic of difficult human issues such as bullying, disempowerment, and anger if not outright rage, often with a root cause of the stigmatized disease of depression.

While not necessarily a cure-all to what ails so many in our society, if we truly desire to grow and expand our world, we must first grow and expand ourselves through the self-discovery of an inner glow and flow that radiates outward into all we think, say, and do.

A yearning for soul depth pulses behind the eyes of our young today, but they need guidance to remember their personal soul truth and encouragement to allow it to emerge, rather than conforming to the dictates of others. For this purpose, I've created the initial framework for a self-love kit. I encourage parents and children alike to work with these offerings. Discuss them, dissect them, collage them, journal them, draw them, express them, and create soul reminders in the form of visual cues with them.

SELF-LOVE Is… Experiencing a greater intimacy with our own soul through inner work, emotional excavation, stillness, presence, and joy.

SELF-LOVE Is… Understanding that we are, first and foremost, powerful, creative, divine, limitless, formless, eternal, infinite beings who co-create reality with the universe according to the energy related to all we think, say, do, believe, and feel.

SELF-LOVE Is… Accepting, claiming, and celebrating the divine paradox that's life. The nature of reality is both-and rather than either-or. Peace is found by resting within the paradox instead of resisting it.

SELF-LOVE Is... Understanding that our truth is personal, powerful, and unique to us, as there are an infinite number of streams that ultimately lead to the glorious sea of oneness.

SELF-LOVE Is... Feeling our way with soul, rather than solely thinking our way through when it comes to making a simple decision or choosing a life path allowing our inner being to captain our ship.

SELF-LOVE Is... Factoring ourselves in at all times, no matter what the circumstance, so that we always live true and thereby offer our highest truth to the world.

SELF-LOVE Is... Embracing our humanity by tenderly and lovingly acknowledging, accepting, and appreciating *all* human experiences as what it means to become consciously soul-embodied, becoming a witness to our story rather than the story itself.

SELF-LOVE Is... Making our overall well-being—emotional, physical, mental, and spiritual—our priority in each and every choice, since everything in our reality stems from it.

SELF-LOVE Is... Consistently making conscious choices that reflect *our* truth, not the truth of another, without apology.

SELF-LOVE Is... Trusting ourselves to know what resonates *for us* in all situations, while simultaneously blessing all else and leaving it for others who are a match.

SELF-LOVE Is... Understanding that our internal perspective in large measure creates our external experience.

SELF-LOVE Is... Allowing ourselves to flow naturally with life by surrendering to what *is,* rather than succumbing to the belief that life ought to be different.

SELF-LOVE Is... Allowing direct divine connection in everyday reality by opening up our unique channels through authentic living.

SELF-LOVE Is... Doing the necessary uncovering of old beliefs and patterns through a variety of self-exploratory means in order to fully know, embrace, and unconditionally love the *man in the mirror* so that wholeness may be felt deep within and thereby expressed in physical reality.

SELF-LOVE Is... Allowing our soul purpose (dharma) to emerge in a way that feels good to us, without resistance or reliance on the approval of others.

SELF-LOVE Is... The freedom to be passionately, fully, unabashedly, and authentically ourselves in every moment of every day.

We are each enough! Self-love, coupled with compassion and loving service toward our fellow humans that stems from our truth, will create both the personal life and world that our hearts truly desire. If encouraged, modeled, and allowed in our young, the mental health issues, as well as much physical dis-ease of our day, will mostly dissipate.

The time is now to snap out of a victim-blame mentality to take full responsibility for both our interior and external worlds, teaching our children through our example to do the same. The time is now to carve out the space to do the inner work that on some level we deeply understand must be faced. Resistance to personal truth and power no longer serves parents, children, or the world at large. The time is now, first to discover our *true* personal power within, and then to offer it passionately *up* and *out* to all.

APPENDIX 2

Pillars of Wisdom for the World of Education

In education today, the knowledge base needs to become secondary to the pillars of wisdom that should be at the heart of teaching. Knowledge would be infused into these pillars and no longer be the near-singular focus it is today. An awareness-based curriculum would invite harmony with the collective, while also encouraging the emergence of individual gifts.

The following ideas could form the basis of a discussion on a new educational focus:

1) Oneness *and* individuation
2) Soul to soul versus role to role
3) Self-awareness and self-love
4) Accountability and responsibility
5) Connectedness *and* boundaries
6) Honesty and transparency
7) Diversity *and* sameness
8) Authenticity and joy
9) The shadow *and* illumination
10) Perspective and truth
11) The intelligent physical body and healing
12) Energy is everything
13) Emotions as guideposts
14) True power and presence
15) Inner world *and* outer world
16) Grow is me rather than woe is me
17) Both-and *and* either-or realities
18) Intuitive knowing
19) Conscious relationships
20) Giving *and* receiving
21) Gratitude as a creative force
22) Mother Earth and grounding
23) Creating reality and the mind
24) Peace *within* the paradoxes
25) Love

APPENDIX 3

Soul to Soul Circles:
Who, What, and Why So Important for All Ages

Many have asked me what a Soul to Soul Circle entails. Circles are nothing new, but rather an ancient form of communication. If done well, they facilitate soul communion, gently pulling back our ego-based masks to allow the inner person to become better known, not only to others but also to themselves.

Individuals of any age group, any culture, can benefit from being part of a Soul to Soul Circle. Whether a teen, a parent, a professional, retired, or elderly, there's a place for you in a Soul to Soul Circle. We want you to come exactly as you are, and we want you to be fully seen and heard.

I have been offering Soul to Soul Circles in a safe and sacred space for over eight years, and with each passing year, realize what a powerful gathering a circle can be. But when I use the word "sacred," I want to be clear that Soul to Soul Circles aren't religious—although my current circles include a rabbi's wife, Catholics, former-Catholics, Unitarians, Jews, members of other faiths, as well as those like myself who don't subscribe to a religion. Labeling in ways that separate is the opposite of what a circle is about. Instead, the point is to break through the layers of the human suit to reach the heart and soul.

It takes courage to join a Soul to Soul Circle. Upon their first foray into this kind of forum, most express some anxiety. There's a fear of being vulnerable—of being truly seen—that brings up hidden facets of one's interior. I appreciate the gumption of any individual who is willing to sit among twenty others and venture beneath the surface of their humanity into the unexplored ocean depths of soul.

There's no one way to run a Soul to Soul Circle. My preference is to select something that serves as a gateway into the soul, typically a book, which is used as the basis of a ten-week series. We meet once a week for two hours. The book is simply a vehicle for inviting self-exploration—a launching pad for self-reflection and the journey into wholeness.

For me, the bottom line when it comes to selecting a book is how it relates to *me*. Is what the author offers true for me? That's my barometer. In other words, does a book *stir my heart to offer more love to both myself and others? Does it deepen my felt experience of oneness? Does it remind me I'm an embodied soul? Is it an impetus to look deep inside myself for personal development, assisting me to integrate my various aspects? Does it inspire greater wholeness within my human experience? Does it assist me in dismantling my ego? Does it ignite in me a greater capacity for non-judgment? Does it help me blend both the physical and soul perspectives to form a single vantage point?* I'm sure by now that you're gathering this isn't your typical book club, and neither is it intended to be.

As for the format, I offer a brief spontaneous invocation of gratitude for all aspects of the circle. We share a few minutes of silence together. We check in with one another on anything that may be on the tip of the tongue and in need of expression—something that occurred during the week, such as a synchronicity or a challenging issue in a participant's life. Then we move into the material, each having brought at least three themes that relate to the above questions in some way. Finally, we end with a tremendous "thank you."

The Soul to Soul Circle isn't in any way, shape, or form a top-down gathering. The attention is not centered on a leader, but rather moves in all directions depending on who's sharing at the moment. As the facilitator, I set the tone and context. In my circles the context is what one might call spiritual development, and the tone is soft, gentle, clear, and deep. It's important to note that, because we are focused on our humanness as an expression of soul, there's much, much humor to be enjoyed!

Our circles have no agenda other than to experience greater intimacy with our own soul, along with witnessing the same in each other. The point is to be able to live more truthfully and fully as whole human beings. From this space, we gradually learn to navigate the world from the vantage point of inner truth—in other words, more from soul and less from role.

Through the circles, our understanding deepens in a number of ways:

- Both teacher and student live within each of us
- Multiple perspectives share the same space
- All relationships and life situations provide an opportunity for personal development
- We are accountable for all that occurs in our own life
- Listening without the need to rescue, save, or "fix" anyone is empowering to all
- We are each connected, and our personal development has a ripple effect on all humanity
- Soul to Soul engagement requires presence, love, compassion, and truth

We are living at a time when an energy shift is occurring, so that aspects of the divine feminine are beginning to merge with the masculine orientation that has dominated for centuries. The Soul to Soul Circle is a representation of this shift and can be utilized across all regions, religions, organizations, and institutions to become a venue for greater self-awareness and authenticity. Circles can be called by any name—such as power circles, presence circles, and truth circles, depending on what floats your boat.

As the facilitator, I recommend an exchange of energy of some kind. I charge for my circles as they are a large part of my work. But the details and vision of a circle will be up to whoever decides to create it. Again, there are no set rules, and all I'm suggesting is a possible framework.

There's much to be gained from this form of communion. I leave you with the following quote from Howard Thurman: *There is something within each of us that waits and listens for the sound of the genuine in the other…and in ourselves.*

In Gratitude

To my parents, sister and in-laws, thank you for the continued support and for loving my children so completely…

To my Soul to Soul Circles, thank you for our sacred time together. Your presence in my life means the world to me…

To Cathy Adams, thank you for our friendship. It's one in a million. There are no words…

To Mike Vecchio, thank you for believing in me so thoroughly. You empower me…

To Linda Nuss and Alexandra Folz, thank you for being such gentle and loving touchstones in my life. You both inspire me…

To Meredith Sinclair, thank you for being that friend who is always up for a little fun. You are very special to me…

To Kimbra Burnside, Becky Flanigan, Laurie Marshall, Susannah Wallenstrom and Sandra Miller, thank you for being lifelong friends. You are each a treasure unto me in your own beautiful way…

To my Facebook friends, thank you for the endless support, encouragement, enthusiasm and laughs. I enjoy sharing my life with you. You are all very dear to me…

To my many teachers along the way, thank you for honoring me just as I am. Your energy infuses these pages…

To Bill Gladstone, thank you for being my literary agent. Your insight is always helpful...

To Nancy Cleary, thank you for choosing to publish both of my books and for all of your efforts on my behalf. I deeply appreciate your belief in my work...

To David Ord, thank you for being such a kind and brilliant editor. I absolutely loved working with you on this book...

To Jim, Aidenn, Piper and Pete, thank you for encouraging me to be unabashedly myself. Sharing my life with the four of you is my greatest blessing. I love you beyond words...

Index

A
acedia, 210, 211
Adams, Cathy Cassani, xvi
anti-bullying, 145. *See also* empathy to true service
Ardagh, Chameli, 176
awakening, 8, 16, 23, 203. *See also* shifts
    acedia, 210, 211
    extroversion, 210–211
    introversion, 210–211
    no self, 22
    oneness, 8, 11
    parenting, 208–209
    paths, 8–9, 11–12
    problems in world, 209
    relationships, 209
    relative vs. absolute truth, 9
    role as barrier, 19
    self-transformation, 20–22
    shedding our false layers, 47
    spiritual community, 45–46
    stages of, 205–206
    triggering catalyst, 24
awareness, 14–15. *See also* back end to front end awareness
    -based curriculum, 216
    ego-based to soul-based, 124

B
back end to front end awareness, 116. *See also* awakening; awareness; shifts
    for children, 123
    creating own reality, 119–120
    energy assessment, 118–120
    energy field and borders, 118–119
    energy flow, 125–126
    focus, 125
    front end work, 116–118
    intuition, 120–123
    modeling for children, 127–128
    parenting, 123–124
    setting an intention, 126
    western women's role, 124–125
being, 85
    stillness of, 88
big love, 172
    experiencing, 174–175
    kinship, 176
    perspective, 177
    realizing the value, 181–182
    self-love and, 180
    Senator Rob Portman and, 175
    soul to soul moments, 178–179
    stepping toward, 180–181
blended being, 201, 203, 211. *See also* physica being to blended being
body-soul simpatico, 57. *See also* outer symptoms to inner signals
Brown, Brene, 110
bullying, 145. *See also* empathy to true service
busyness without to stillness within, 83. *See also* awakening; shifts
    being and doing, 85–88
    busyness, 83–85
    Costco run, 89
    creative process, 86–87
    downtime, 92
    honing process, 84
    non-action periods, 87
    non-stop busyness, 89–90
    reflection and contemplation, 85
    role and identity, 92–93
    silence, 88–89
    stillness, 88
    travel sports, 90–92
butterfly mom's perspective, 112. *See also* striving to contentment

C
capitalized entity, 156
Chopra, Deepak, 56
circles, 217
Collins, Jason, 105
compassion, 141–142, 143, 146–148. *See also* empathy
conscious, 14–15
contentment, 109. *See also* striving to contentment
Crow, Sheryl, 111

D
Dass, Ram, 106, 107
Dave Matthews Band, 199–200
Dalai Lama, 124
diminishment to mutuality, 149. *See also* awakening; shifts
    appreciating ourselves, 157–158
    capitalized entity, 156
    comparison and competition, 153–154
    comparison with others, 151
    criticisms, 154
    dualism, 156
    oneness, 155, 156
    qualification and identity, 158–159
    self-doubt, 151
    social media, 160–161
    soul, 155
    spirit, 155
    teacher and student, 151–153
doing, 85–88. *See also* busyness without to stillness within
dualism, 156.

Duncan, Michael Clarke, 14

E

ego, 14–15. *See also* awakening; awareness; human roles; self-betrayal to self-love
    based to soul-based awareness, 124
    and defined paths, 46
    emancipation, 46
    inversion, 132
Einstein, 89
emotional baggage, 114. *See also* striving to contentment
emotional triggers, 74. *See also* woe is me to grow is me
    dealing, 75–78
    shadow work, 78
empathy, 139. *See also* empathy to true service
    boy and butterfly, 140–141
    compassion, 141–142, 143, 146–148
    Psyche and Aphrodite myth, 144
    self-denying, 142–144
    trap of extreme, 140–142
empathy to true service, 138. *See also* awakening; empathy; shifts
    anti-bullying and pro-acceptance, 145–146
    bullying, 145
    compassion, 141–142, 143, 146–148
    energy exchange, 145
    service to another, 139–140
empowerment, 96
energy flow, 125–126. *See also* back end to front end awareness
extrovert, 210, 211

F

feeling our way, 51–53. *See also* path to no path
feelings, 74–75
focus, 125. *See also* back end to front end awareness
forgiveness, 81. *See also* woe is me to grow is me
front end responsibility, 116. *See also* back end to front end awareness
front end ways of living, 116. *See also* back end to front end awareness

G

gateways, 96, 99–101. *See also* hiding to self-expression
    cyber friendships, 102–103
    internal reality, 98
    promoting pursuit of, 101
    self-care importance, 98
    to self-expression, 97
    social media, 101–104
Gandhi, 139, 176

Green Mile, The, 13
Grow is Me perspective, 73. *See also* woe is me to grow is me
Grow is Me rather than Woe is Me. *See* woe is me to grow is me

H

hiding to self-expression, 94. *See also* awakening; gateways; shifts
    being true to ourselves, 105–106
    empowerment, 96
    feeling your own way, 106–107
    joyful self-expression, 95–96
    preferences, 104–105
    self-exploratory journey, 95
high school reunion, 78
honing, 84. *See also* busyness without to stillness within
human roles, 16. *See also* ego
    as barrier, 19
    closets, 18
    disposing, 18
    perceptions, 17
    to soul, 15–18
humanity, 209
humility, 131–134. *See also* self-betrayal to self-love

I

I Am, 19
individuation to oneness, 183. *See also* awakening; oneness; shifts
    internal knowing, 184–185
    pointillism, 186
    separation thinking, 186–187
    soul to soul relationship, 192–193
    soul union, 191–193
integration, 6–7. *See also* peace
introvert, 210
intuition, 120. *See also* back end to

J

Jacobson, Leonard, 195
Jesus, 37, 92–93, 131, 139, 176

K

King, Martin Luther, 139, 176

L

Lao-Tzu, 20, 81
Lazarus, 92
little to big love, 172. *See also* awakening; big love; shifts
    kinship, 176
    raising children, 176
Lesser, Elizabeth, 54

M

Mandela, Nelson, 176
Mckenna, Jed, 44
meditation. *See* silence

mental health, 213
message, 208
messenger, 207–208
Milk, Harvey, 18
Morrison, Van, 118
Mother Teresa, 172, 176

N
negative emotion, 58
Nautilus award, 154
New Age, 198–199. *See also* physical being to blended being
no path, 44. *See also* path to no path
no self, 22. *See also* awakening
non-stop busyness, 89–90. *See also* busyness without to stillness within

O
First Lady Michelle Obama, 166
Oliver, Mary, 83
oneness, 8, 11, 155, 156, 206–207. *See also* big love; individuation to oneness
   after death, 191
   everyone as part of, 173–174
   expressions of, 185–186
   life and death, 188–191
   necessity to teach, 193–194
   in two individuated souls, 187–188
ourselves, 3
outer symptoms to inner signals, 54. *See also* awakening; shifts
   body as intelligent system, 56–59
   body awareness 61–62
   body-soul simpatico, 57
   challenges, 66–68
   conscious on thoughts, 70–71
   dis-ease, 57
   exposing hidden aspects of ourselves, 58
   identification and attachment, 68–70
   perspective change, 59–61
   physical ailments and soul, 55
   relationship with myself, 59
   self-exploration, 60
   self-healing, 56
   symptoms, 56, 58, 62–66

P
parent-child relationship, 80–82. *See also* woe is me to grow is me
parenting, 123–124, 208–209
Parker, Lonnae O'Neal, 166
path to no path, 44. *See also* awakening; shifts
   beliefs and paths, 48
   complexity vs. simplicity, 45
   feeling our way, 51–53
   restrictive qualifiers, 49
   role to soul, 48–51
   soul identification, 49–51
   spiritual community, 45–46
   true freedom, 47–48
   voice of soul, 52
paths, 8–9, 46, 206
   aspects of, 47
   finding, 11–12
   no path, 44
peace, 2
   in paradox 24
   soul, 4–6
   view of ourselves, 3
   we, 5
   wholeness, 3
physical ailments and soul, 55. *See also* outer symptoms to inner signals
physical being to blended being, 195. *See also* awakening; shifts
   acknowledgment and appreciation, 202
   awakening, 203
   choices and blended being, 201
   Dave Matthews Band, 199–200
   integrity, 201
   in love with soul, 201–204
   New Age, 198–199
   pains of world, 195–198
   Prophecy of the Condor and the Eagle, 204
   religion and spirituality, 200
pillars of wisdom, 216
Plato, 54
pointillism, 186. *See also* individuation to oneness
problems in world, 209
Prophecy of the Condor and the Eagle, the, 204
Po, Huang, 162

R
relationships, 209. *See also* outer symptoms to inner signals
   with myself, 59
   and personal development, 137
relative truth, 10
Remen, Rachel Naomi, M.D., 57
resisting to resting within paradoxes, 162. *See also* awakening; shifts
   acceptance of perspectives, 166
   acquiring peace, 165
   being wholeness, 163–165
   dichotomies, 163
   divine paradox, 167
   sacredness, 167–169
   spiritual practice, 169–171
role to soul, 33. *See also* awakening; shifts
   awakening and changes, 35–37
   expressing ultimate oneness, 37–40
   external and inner life, 34
   out from psychic debris, 40–43

priority and choices, 34
Roshi, Yasutani, 183

S

seeker, 1–2. *See also* awakening; diminishment to mutuality; hiding to self-expression; self-betrayal to self-love; outer symptoms to inner signals; shadow work
    betrayals, 130–131
    doubt, 151
    exploration, 60
    exploratory journey, 95
    expression, 95
    healing, 56
    love, 129
    love and big love, 180
    love kit, 213–215
    transformation, 20–22
    validation, 137
self-betrayal to self-love, 129. *See also* awakening; shifts
    boundary creation, 129
    connection to soul, 134–136
    ego-inversion, 132
    energy of love and integrity, 130
    humility, 131–134
    relationships, 137
    self-betrayals, 130–131
    self-love, 129
    self-validation, 137
Self-Love Kit, 213
Senator Rob Portman, 175
separation thinking, 186–187. *See also* individuation to oneness
service to another, 139–140. *See also* empathy to true service
setting an intention, 126. *See also* back end to front end awareness
Seurat, 186
shadow work, 73, 78. *See also* self-exploratory journey
shifts, 23. *See also* awakening
    fifteen shifts, 25
    unconscious, 27
    unique path, 26–27
    watching ourselves, 28–30
silence, 88–89. *See also* busyness without to stillness within
soul, 4, 155. *See also* striving to contentment
    arena, 109–111
    communion, 20
    concepts, 5–6
    role to, 15–18
    unforgetting, 16
Soul to Soul Circle, 217
    agenda, 219
    energy shift, 219–220
    gateway to soul, 218
    ways of understanding, 219

spirit, 155
spiritual activism and service, 208
spiritual bypass, 209
spiritual path, the, 155
spirituality, 200
stillness, 88. *See also* busyness without to stillness within
striving to contentment, 108. *See also* awakening; shifts
    butterfly mom's perspective, 112
    emotional baggage, 114
    energy beings, 114
    soul arena, 109–111
    success, 111
    tiger moms vs. butterfly moms, 111–113
    weight maintenance, 113–115
striving, 108–109.
success, 111. *See also* striving to contentment

T

teen suicide, 193
Tiger Mom, 111
Thailand, 181
Thoreau, Henry David, 205
Thurman, Howard, 220
truth, 10. *See also* I Am

U

unforgetting, 16
unstructured time, 92. *See also* busyness without to stillness within

V

view of ourselves, 3

W

Walsch, Neale Donald, 171
Whitman, Walt, 149
western woman, 124–125
wholeness, 3, 7, 47, 206–207. *See also* soul
wisdom, 216
woe is me to grow is me, 72. *See also* awakening; shifts
    becoming clear mirror, 80–81
    emotional triggers, 74, 75–78
    feeling energy pattern, 78–80
    feelings, 74–75
    forgiveness, 81
    Grow is Me perspective, 73
    parent-child relationship, 80–82
    shadow work, 73, 78

ABOUT THE AUTHOR

Annie Burnside is a bridge between relative and absolute truth. Her work helps others integrate a new perspective—a blended one—that expands the lens through which they view the world. Her first book, *Soul to Soul Parenting*, won the 2011 Nautilus Silver Book Award. *From Role to Soul* is her second book. Annie facilitates Soul to Soul Circles and offers private soul nurturing sessions where she lives in Chicago, Illinois with her husband and three children.

www.annieburnside.com

www.ingramcontent.com/pod-product-compliance
Lightning Source LLC
Chambersburg PA
CBHW071657090426
42738CB00009B/1568